$7.95

The Educated Woman

Prospects and Problems

The past ten years reflect a raised public consciousness about the role of women in the United States, a role in the process of changing. In contemplating her future, the educated woman today is confronted by uncertainty, conflicting pressures, and often false expectations.

The impression that qualified women are very willing to sacrifice career aspirations for marriage and a family is largely incorrect, and such willingness as there is seems in part due to the widespread social attitudes implying that it is wrong to make any other kind of choice. Women are raised to believe in their own inferiority and to accept a subordinate status in society.

A discerning look by the authors at women's suffrage and the "quiet years" preceding reemergence of the struggle for equality in the form of Women's Liberation reveals that more cooperative patterns of living are being explored today by younger couples, who are sharing the many tasks of a family menage — one in which children are raised by active parental collaboration, with the father accepting a daily allotment of chores formerly con-

sidered "for women only." Thus the feminine-masculine axis comes up for examination as the concepts and stereotypes of "femininity" and "masculinity" are probed.

In the opinion of the authors, the obdurate inflexibility of the U.S. Establishment must give way if the nation is to profit from the education of its female citizens. Our institutions and industries can and must make concrete adjustments to accommodate the real, rather than the stereotyped, differences between men and women. Only in this way will it be possible for women to meet their marital and maternal obligations to family life while at the same time contributing to the viability of the nation and attaining their own fulfillment.

THE GROUP FOR THE ADVANCEMENT OF PSYCHIATRY (GAP) has a membership of approximately 300 distinguished psychiatrists, most of whom are organized into working committees which devote their efforts toward the study of various aspects of psychiatry. GAP is also the author of *Joys and Sorrows of Parenthood, Normal Adolescence, The Right to Abortion, Drug Misuse, The VIP with Psychiatric Impairment,* and *Humane Reproduction.*

THE
EDUCATED
WOMAN

Prospects and Problems

Formulated by the Committee on the College Student
GROUP FOR THE ADVANCEMENT OF PSYCHIATRY

CHARLES SCRIBNER'S SONS · NEW YORK

Library of Congress Cataloging in Publication Data

Group for the Advancement of Psychiatry. Committee on
the College Student.
The educated woman: prospects and problems.

Bibliography: p.
Includes index.
1. Women—Social conditions—United States.
2. Education of women—United States. 3. College
graduates—Employment—United States. 4. Women—
Psychology. I. Title.
HQ1426.G84 1975   301.41'2   75-2372
ISBN 0-684-14211-2

STATEMENT OF PURPOSE

The Group for the Advancement of Psychiatry has a membership of approximately 300 psychiatrists, most of whom are organized in the form of a number of working committees. These committees direct their efforts toward the study of various aspects of psychiatry and the application of this knowledge to the fields of mental health and human relations.

Collaboration with specialists in other disciplines has been and is one of GAP's working principles. Since the formation of GAP in 1946 its members have worked closely with such other specialists as anthropologists, biologists, economists, statisticians, educators, lawyers, nurses, psychologists, sociologists, social workers, and experts in mass communication, philosophy, and semantics. GAP envisages a continuing program of work according to the following aims:

1. To collect and appraise significant data in the fields of psychiatry, mental health, and human relations

5

2. To reevaluate old concepts and to develop and test new ones
3. To apply the knowledge thus obtained for the promotion of mental health and good human relations

GAP is an independent group, and its reports represent the composite findings and opinions of its members only, guided by its many consultants.

The Educated Woman: Prospects and Problems was formulated by the Committee on the College Student. The contributions of a former committee member, various consultants, and others are recognized in the Acknowledgments. The current members of this committee, as well as other committees and the officers of GAP, are listed at the end of the book.

ACKNOWLEDGMENTS

The Committee is particularly grateful to our consultants: Elga R. Wasserman and Joseph Katz contributed significantly to the writing of the book; Alice S. Rossi gave thoughtful and constructive criticism, which was invaluable in the formative period; and Kenneth Keniston provided extraordinarily useful and penetrating editorial comment. We are also greatly indebted to two pairs of Ginsburg Fellows: Clay C. Whitehead and Marlin Mattson were extremely helpful in the initial stages of conception and writing, and Harris Rabinovich and Allan I. Bezan were equally helpful in the later stages of reorganizing and sharpening the focus of the book in its final form.

In the preparation of the manuscript we were greatly aided by the Maurice Falk Medical Fund, which contributed generously to the costs of manuscript reproduction, and by Philip B. Hallen, President of the Falk Fund, whose encouragement, advice, and personal support were always available when needed.

The tedious chore of typing and proofreading draft revisions was cheerfully done by members of the Division of Mental Hygiene, Yale University Health Services, clerical and administrative staff: Lucy Cunningham, Marie Meneely, Mary Petrini, Ann Bishop, Doris Shumway, and Janet Rozen.

Finally, we would like to acknowledge our debt to Alfred Flarsheim, a committee member for many years, who participated in the early formulation of the report but retired from the committee before its completion.

CONTENTS

9

CONTENTS

THE EDUCATED WOMAN
Prospects and Problems

one INTRODUCTION

Women in college contemplating their futures are confronted today by uncertainty, conflicting pressures, and often false expectations. The author of a recent article in a popular magazine, describing her life immediately after college, said that she got married, had a baby, got divorced, and spent the next years "growing up." She commented that she felt "the sequence was wrong," and she hoped that the current generation of college women would not suffer the same difficulties.[1]

The past ten years have been marked by a rising concern and "raised consciousness" with regard to the role of women in the United States, the consequences of which may affect some of the most important patterns of living. The members of the Committee on the College Student of the Group for the Advancement of Psychiatry were particularly aware of these issues, because on campuses generally there has been much discussion about women's future roles, opportunities, and relationships, and as psychiatrists dealing with women students in clinical settings, they found them frequently a subject of concern. This book is an attempt to define the situation of the college woman and the problems she faces today.

A college woman in her junior or senior year is in the throes of making decisions that will inevitably affect her entire future—in other words, she is thinking about the pattern of her life after graduation: career, marriage, family, and so on. Consider the rather poignant case of the woman just mentioned, who found that issues she did not resolve in college or shortly thereafter came back to haunt her fifteen years later. If she could somehow have been helped to change the sequence and do it "the right way around"—whatever that might have been for her as an individual —she would clearly have achieved more satisfying personal fulfillment at the cost of considerably less suffering.

The following statement of one student's feelings is an example of many college women's sense of genuine conflict and uncertainty about their future.

Having rejected the option of immediately continuing on in school, I have been feeling at times a dread which is close to paralyzing—for there seems to be a near-vacuum of available resources of guidance for women intending to go out into the world directly from Ivy, to support themselves.

Ivy seems to foist a kind of guilt on one who chooses this option. I would tend to think that the guilt may be more strongly felt by women here, for the trite notion of *noblesse oblige* on the part of women here is not to be underestimated. It would seem that the bulk of the energies directed by Ivy at graduating seniors is toward helping them continue on in their education, and where energies are directed toward helping students find employment, it is an understatement to say that these opportunities are overwhelmingly male-oriented.

Second point: A senior male friend of mine commented to me the other day, "If I'm going to be a policeman, I'm going to be chief of the police force—if I'm going to be a professor, I'm going to be an Ivy professor." *Ivy men largely leave here with the feeling that whatever they eventually undertake, they will be the leaders, at the top, in control, and accomplish something significant.* Whatever the emphasis on 1000 male leaders per year, this type of indoctrination has an unmistakable corollary effect on their women counterparts. I feel that it would be difficult for me to be truly happy in a career position where there was no opportunity to exercise some type of creative leadership. It is acceptable socially and intellectually (indeed expected) that the woman graduate of many colleges take a job as a junior editor with Harper & Row or as a junior researcher for Time-Life—positions that are often more skin than bones, both intellectually and monetarily. But what does it mean for an Ivy woman to "make it"?

Which leads to point number three: Are our role models for "making it" to be, as they seem to have been thus far, those of the men? Or will we be able to develop distinctive goals and means of our own, as I believe we must? Many of the women I know who graduated from Ivy last year are at law schools, graduate schools, business schools—and many of the reasons for their choices seem to be closely related to wanting to "make it" as an Ivy man might "make it." I am not denigrating the option of continuing school—I am simply attempting to deal with the plausibility of other alternatives for the near future. Those women I know who are out holding jobs seem to be suffering a painful identity crisis: "Should I be doing something more, something better? Is *this* what my Ivy education had led me to?"

This statement indicates some of the real discrepancies among individual ambitions, the expectations of others, and the realistic possibilities. It also reveals the uncertainties and the burdens imposed by having choices available. Often, the most that can be done for a student in such a predicament is to try to help her clarify the sources of her confusion, some of which come from conflicts within herself, and some of which arise from her accurate view of social conditions for women.

Personal conflicts seem to limit choices for women more than they do for men—for example, conflicts related to achievement often make it difficult for women to strive for success. In addition, women have to deal with the ambivalent attitude of society toward them, and particularly toward women who seek careers.

Many of these problems are inseparable from those faced by anyone becoming an adult, but in our opinion women face specific problems that are particularly intense in this era when sex roles and family patterns are changing.

Because of the attitudes of other people, the woman who considers a career involving a major investment of time outside the home may feel that her femininity is in question. If she wants to work during the childbearing years, her uncertainty is even greater, for most people in the United States today place a great deal of emphasis on the mother's remaining at home and acting as the central housekeeper in the family. One often hears that qualified women are very willing to sacrifice career aspirations in favor of marriage and family, but surely these women are influenced by widespread social attitudes which imply that it is wrong to make any other choice. This conclusion is frequently justified on the basis of "the biologically determined character of women," and these attitudes about the "appropriate" concerns of women are reinforced daily by the media. Take, for example, the following television commercial:

"Mother, for a while this morning, I thought I wasn't cut out for married life. Hank was late for work and forgot his apricot juice and walked out without kissing me, and when I was all alone I started crying. But then the postman came with the sheets and towels you sent, that look like big bandanna handkerchiefs, and you know what I thought? That those big red and blue handkerchiefs are for girls like me to dry their tears on so they can get busy and do what a housewife has to do. Throw open the windows and start getting the house ready, and the dinner, maybe clean the silver and put new geraniums in the box. Everything to be ready for him when he walks through the door."

The assumption that women should be exclusively loving wives and mothers is more widely shared by teachers, parents, and employers than one might anticipate and exerts a tremendous impact on the way women view themselves, how they are raised, and what is expected of them. In many important respects, most people behave the way they are expected to behave. Women are raised to believe in their own inferiority and to accept a subordinate status in society. The dynamics may be similar to those of minority groups such as blacks, even though women are not numerically a minority. It is not surprising, then, that in the face of peer-group pressures, cultural norms, parental training, and teachers' expectations women are so often in conflict about achievement in adult realms other than the home. In a recent study, college women were asked to rate a series of professional articles.[2] For the purpose of the experiment, identical sets of articles were attributed to male and female authors. The respondents consistently rated articles signed by men as better in terms of style and content than the same articles attributed to women.

This book focuses on the woman's life plan in the broadest sense and is not restricted to such problems as whether a woman can successfully function as both a wife and a professional, or which professions are most practical for a woman to consider. These problems are discussed only as part of the basic dilemma.

A book about women must also consider the role of men, because women cannot be isolated from their social context and this includes as one critical component the male-female relationship. If one partner in a relationship changes, the other will of necessity change also. The following case illustrates this point:

Heidi and Jim were living together. Both were students in the same college. Jim was planning to work for a while after graduation, Heidi to attend graduate school. They did not feel prepared to get married. She looked forward to graduation, which had the symbolic meaning of freeing her from a domineering, controlling family.

Although Heidi and Jim knew that contraceptive counseling was available, they "never got around to" doing anything about it. Just before graduation Heidi realized she was pregnant. She felt enormous guilt, and in conflict about what to do. She began to argue with

Jim, was unable to complete her work, and became depressed. Although very much interested in the graduate English program in which she had been accepted, she felt that to put her work above a family would be "wrong."

Heidi felt caught between her conscious wish for independence from her family and autonomy in her relationship with Jim, and her fear about what this would involve. She went to a counselor for help in deciding what to do. In the course of counseling she recognized that in part her pregnancy was a way of dealing with her fear of going out into the world (of graduate school). This led her to become aware of her deeper dependency wishes. These insights made it easier for her to defer marriage and decide to have an abortion. As she discussed some of these feelings with Jim, he recognized that he had encouraged her dependency because it increased his feeling of masculinity. Unconsciously he had wanted the pregnancy to prove to himself his ability to be a father, and for this reason did not urge an abortion, although he realized that it was the "sensible" course of action. Eventually, when both Heidi and Jim felt more established emotionally, they found their relationship to be more solidly based.

The educated woman faces a dilemma that admits of no easy solution. In this book the Committee hopes to clarify some of the dimensions of the dilemma and to provide information that may help individual college students to sort out some of their conflicts and uncertainties.

two   A HISTORICAL PERSPECTIVE

The widespread preoccupation with the position of women in Western society that emerged during the 1960s was not a sudden development, but had roots which, in the United States, can be traced back for at least a hundred and fifty years. The attempt of women to achieve equality with men has progressed unevenly in a number of areas, and it has been attended by varying degrees of resistance on the part of society at large.[1] Particular movements, such as the woman suffrage movement, or the women's rights movement, have been paralleled by, and often intertwined with, movements designed to gain equality for other groups. In the 1960s the upsurge of concern and action commonly referred to as Women's Liberation raised crucial issues about the role and place of women in our society and inevitably had an impact on college women. No comprehensive history can be given here, but a few remarks will provide some background and perspective for the current concerns of college women.

In European society women occasionally held positions of power or prominence by virtue of birth (as royalty in England, for example), connections (as mistresses of important men), or talent (as writers, for instance, in Victorian England), but the pioneer society of this country clearly viewed them as "the weaker, the inferior sex. Their position in marriage was distinctly subordinate—their chief duty being 'obedience' to their husbands. Their mental and moral capacities were rated well below those of men." [2] In most instances, laws were based on English models and women had few rights. For example, women were not allowed to own land or to vote. Their role in the family, however, gave them a real function in society that a later technology made less essential.

In an agrarian society men and women shared jointly in the economic and social life of the communities in which they lived. Women participated in the production of food, manufacture of clothing, care of the sick, teaching of the young, and management of the home. They performed a multitude of tasks beyond those of bearing and rearing children. Although they were not paid for these tasks, often the men were not paid either, in the sense of receiving a salary, but the product of the labor of the entire family was sold. Furthermore, in Colonial America the scarcity of women enhanced their value.

During the nineteenth century the industrial revolution, which created a host of transformations, vitally changed the living patterns of both men and women. It caused a gradual shift for men from agriculture to industrial labor, which brought with it a move from the farm to the city. This change meant, first, that women could at times compete for jobs in industry, and, second, that many traditionally homemade products were replaced by factory-produced goods or commercially processed foods. Household tasks became less time-consuming for middle-class women, and their energy was freed for activities outside the home, such as study, volunteer work, jobs, political activity, and social reform.[3]

Opposed to this trend was another—the Victorian emphasis on the sanctity of the home and hearth "as the fount of all the tender virtues in life." [4] When women were regarded as goddesses of the hearth, they may have gained some reverence, but they also were confined to the home.

The fight for education for women progressed slowly. Not until the latter part of the eighteenth century were secondary schools available to girls, and admission of women to colleges came later still.[5] In the early part of the nineteenth century several of the better women's seminaries provided an education approaching in quality that of men's colleges, and later some of them attained collegiate rank—notably Mount Holyoke, founded as a seminary in 1837. Oberlin College was years ahead of the times in its encouragement of women, offering them admission in 1837, but it was not until mid-century that women's colleges appeared—in 1855, Elmira, and in 1865, Vassar. They were followed by Smith, Wellesley, and Bryn Mawr. In 1852 Antioch followed Oberlin's lead and became coeducational, as did Cornell. The passage in 1862 of the Land Grant Act, which authorized grants of land for state agricultural colleges, and the subsequent strengthening of state universities, considerably increased the opportunities for women, because most state universities were coeducational from the beginning or became so rather rapidly. In the latter part of the century several women's colleges (Pembroke, Jackson, Barnard, Radcliffe) were opened as affiliates of established men's colleges.

By 1900, therefore, women had made some progress in attaining college education, but their admission to the professions was to be still further delayed.[6] Elizabeth Blackwell, later hailed as the first woman physician, obtained a medical degree against odds from Geneva Medical College in 1849, but was forced to go abroad for advanced training. In 1850 and 1852, however, special schools for medical training for women were started in Philadelphia and Boston. By 1891 there were 1300 women in medical training, compared with more than 18,000 men. Progress in law was equally slow or slower. In 1900 there were 151 women law students and 12,365 men.

In graduate schools proper, the story was somewhat better— approximately 40 per cent of graduate students in 1900 were women. Only in teaching and nursing were significantly more women than men admitted. In teaching this was partly caused by the heavy male Civil War casualties, which necessitated attracting women to fill open positions.[7] The teacher-training institutions were seminaries and normal schools. By 1900 there were twice as many women as men preparing to be teachers. Initially nursing schools were almost always attached to hospitals and so provided a somewhat different educational experience from that prevailing in other fields. From the beginning nursing was predominantly a woman's profession.

Political activity was a second important area for women, and one in which they participated vigorously, sometimes on their own behalf and sometimes on behalf of others. The woman suffrage movement is usually dated from 1848, when a group of women who had become acquainted with one another in anti-slavery campaigns held a meeting. The idea for the meeting was conceived, appropriately, at a Friends' Yearly Meeting; the Quakers had always recognized the equal rights of women.

Lucretia Mott, Elizabeth Cady Stanton, Lucy Stone, Carrie Chapman Catt, and Susan B. Anthony were all leaders in the woman suffrage movement. The fight was long and slow, but, one by one, individual states enfranchised women. Finally, in 1919, a Constitutional amendment which stated that "the right to vote . . . shall not be denied or abridged . . . on account of sex" passed both Houses of Congress and was ratified by the required number of states in 1920 to become the Nineteenth Amendment.

Meanwhile, in a few isolated areas other legal gains had been made. In 1850 Oregon permitted single and married women to own land, a concession that has been attributed to the scarcity of women on the frontier and their consequent high status. In general, however, the nineteenth century saw few changes in the legal position of women.[8]

High moral purpose was a common characteristic of the nineteenth-century United States, where people believed deeply in progress and the march of civilization. The role of social reformer was often taken by women, who were considered the more "civilized" sex and who also had less at stake in the business world. The relation between this role and the education of women is eloquently expressed in the will of Sophia Smith, who in leaving money for the founding of Smith College in Massachusetts stated her hope that through education for women "what are called their 'wrongs' will be redressed, their wages adjusted, their weight of influence in reforming evils of society will be greatly increased as teachers, as writers, as mothers, as members of society, their power for good will be incalculably enlarged." [9]

Although their number was not great, women leaders had emerged in many fields by the end of the nineteenth century: Dorothea Dix in hospital reform, Jane Addams in settlement-house work, Clara Barton and Lillian D. Wald in nursing, Ida R. Tarbell in journalism, Charlotte Perkins Gilman in sociology, Frances Willard in temperance work, Harriet Beecher Stowe and Emily Dickinson in literature, M. Carey Thomas in education, and Mary Baker Eddy in religion. There were many vigorous and often militant women working for temperance, public parks, and elimination of prostitution and child labor. In 1953 the historian Richard B. Morris of Columbia University compiled a list of three hundred notable Americans, grouped by category; the only category in which women outnumbered men was that of "Social Reform and Labor Leader." [10]

One result of the industrial revolution was large-scale employment of women and children to meet the demands created by the rapid growth of industry. From the employer's standpoint such labor had the added advantage that it could be hired at a lower wage than adult male labor. Perhaps as a consequence, women were early involved in the labor movement. In the first half of the nineteenth century Sarah Bagley, a mill worker, attempted with some success to organize women. Progress was slow, however, until the end of the century, when the International Ladies Garment Workers Union organized them widely. In the early part of the twentieth century, inspired by the work of the British labor reformer Emmeline Pankhurst, the trade-union movement and the suffrage movement joined and together mounted a series of effective strikes. These strikes, however, advanced the cause of labor rather than that of women, and women workers continued to receive lower pay than men.[11]

At the same time broad social changes that increased the freedom of women were taking place. Customs limiting their independence, fashions in dress, and attitudes toward sexual behavior were changing. The Victorian attitude about female sexuality was that women of the upper and middle classes had no interest in, or enjoyment of, sex. Only lower-class women (i.e., depraved women or prostitutes) were thought to engage in sex with anything but distaste or a sense of marital duty.[12] This belief was in a sense related to Darwin's theory of evolution. The process of evolution was identified with that of social advancement, so that the lower classes were felt to be closest to animals—that is, they had not evolved as far as the upper classes and therefore had more of an "animalistic" nature. How this theory accounted for the sexual proclivities of men is not clear, but presumably upper-class women were the most "civilized" of human beings and hence showed the least interest in sex.

These concepts about female sexuality began to weaken as objective medical observations were recorded, particularly in the writings of Freud and Havelock Ellis. Although currently Freud is a target of attack by feminists, he was in large measure responsible for recognition in the world of science of the importance of sexual pleasure for women. Indeed, his initial descriptions of psychiatric illness in women related it to the lack of appropriate outlets for sexual impulses.[13] Hysteria, a common illness in women of his day, was found to be related to repressed sexual impulses and was cured by "lifting the repression."

Furthermore, Freud took his women patients seriously. His writings and those of his followers had a tremendous influence on attitudes toward women's sexuality for the next seventy years.

The first decade of the twentieth century, then, saw some relaxation of Victorian attitudes, and World War I greatly quickened the tempo of change. The 1920s brought further social liberation and a considerable shift in sexual attitudes. Participation by women in athletics, the opening up of new job areas, changes in dress, acceptance of public smoking and drinking by women— all combined to shatter the Victorian image of the woman as a frail flower that must be protected. (This image had always been reserved for upper- or middle-class women and was somehow preserved, while lower-class women were considered capable of working long hours at arduous tasks, whether in factories or in domestic service.)

In 1916 Margaret Sanger opened her first birth-control clinic, and although she was jailed for it, she continued the fight for family planning.[14] The American judge Ben Lindsey in *Companionate Marriage*[15] and the British philosopher Bertrand Russell in *Marriage and Morals*[16] suggested far-reaching innovations in social arrangements that would affect such previously sacred matters as marriage and the family or forbidden activities such as premarital sexual relationships. Although the views of these people were not generally accepted, their appearance in public print indicates the great change that had occurred. Dress in this period changed conspicuously: greatly shortened skirts, fewer underclothes, and extremely short hair increased women's freedom of movement. At the same time, the automobile increased the geographic mobility of both sexes and also influenced patterns of male-female relationships by providing the complete privacy it had previously been difficult to find.

The 1920s were followed by the Great Depression of the 1930s, during which women of all classes were forced to work outside the home, often because they could find jobs when men could not. However unwillingly they may have accepted this economic necessity, it gave them a further taste of independence. At the same time the development of labor-saving devices made housekeeping something less than a full-time job for women without children. Women began to take an active part in the formal political structure. Several were elected to Congress, one or two became governors, and in 1933 Frances Perkins became the first woman appointed to the United States Cabinet.[17] Although the changes in sexual mores were not as dramatic, the trend started in the 1920s continued. Late in the 1930s improved contraceptives and the discovery of sulfa drugs reduced fears of pregnancy and venereal disease.

During World War II larger numbers of women than ever accepted jobs outside the home, for there was a great demand for their services, and all sorts of accommodations, such as day-care facilities, were worked out to release them from home duties and child care. With the tremendous explosion of technological advances after the war, almost everyone in the middle class could own the major home appliances that took so little time to operate. Developments in the food industry multiplied the number of "convenience foods" and further reduced the time required to run a home. No longer were the roles of wife and mother the long-term full-time commitment they had been. Constraints on women to remain at home decreased. At the same time, many women who had chosen to be simply wives and mothers found that the roles gave little satisfaction. Eventually their assignment to women as primary occupations began to be reconsidered.

Furthermore, the medical advances of the earlier part of the century began to have far-reaching social effects. There was some increase in longevity, particularly for women, and a decrease in infant mortality. Improved methods of family planning, and the high cost of raising children during the Depression years, had effected a reduction in the number of children per family, at least in the middle and upper classes. Although there was a great increase in the birthrate following World War II, the means were available to limit family size and permit spacing of children, while the improved rates of infant survival decreased the number of pregnancies necessary to attain a family of the desired size. Perhaps the single most important factor giving women control over their lives was the development of safe, relatively effective methods of contraception which could be used at the discretion of the woman. For the first time, a woman might have completed her family by the age of twenty-four or younger, and be finished with the most demanding years of child-rearing by forty. She then had approximately thirty years of life ahead without children to care for and must fill her days with other activities.[18]

At the same time, however, Freud's dictum that the presence of the mother was essential for the later healthy personality development of the young child was receiving widespread acceptance. Many of Freud's case histories dwelt on improper child care by the nursemaids who served the middle-class families from which the majority of his patients were drawn. The implication was clear that inadequate "mothering" caused severe psychological disturbance. Later psychoanalytic writing recognized the importance of the child's ability to separate from the mother, but this concept received less popular attention.

Since Freudian ideas were particularly prevalent between the two World Wars, women of the generation that came of age in the 1940s were determined to avoid what they felt were the mistakes of their parents by providing consistent, loving, available mothering to their children. Other studies[19] also depicted the institutionalized child as stunted emotionally, intellectually, and physically, and many middle-class parents drew the conclusion that women should stay at home. Perhaps this decision also satisfied a need for security after the disruptions of the Depression and World War II.

By the time the United States had recovered from World War II, middle-class women attended college almost as a matter of course, and, as the emphasis on credentials escalated, a B.A. became a necessity for getting an interesting job. Nevertheless, the reasons for attending college were not the same for women as for men. College was not automatically thought to be preparation for a woman's career, and the number of women in professions continued to lag. The number of women in law and medicine did not significantly increase until the mid-1960s.[20]

The beginning of the "new" feminist movement of the 1960s is variously ascribed. Some cite the French writer Simone de Beauvoir's *The Second Sex*, published in 1953 in the United States (in 1949 in France), as the starting point.[21] Others, however, feel that de Beauvoir's book really signaled the end of the preceding phase, and that the appointment and report of President Kennedy's Commission on the Status of Women in 1963 was more significant for the future.[22] Still others suggest that the civil rights movement drew women's attention to their own position as an oppressed class. The lessons learned from the Civil Rights demonstrations were seen as applicable in effecting change in attitudes toward women as well as toward Blacks. The American feminist Betty Friedan's *The Feminine Mystique*, published in 1963, was for many the beginning of the movement.[23] The formation in 1966 of the National Organization for Women gave a structure to the strivings of individual women. An influential issue of the journal *Daedalus* (1964) entitled "The Woman in America" [24] provided important intellectual material, and *Sexual Politics* by the American feminist Kate Millett, published in 1970, also received widespread attention.[25]

These several currents had flowed together by the late 1960s, when a full-blown feminist movement emerged. Other demographic factors contributed. For example, in the mid-1960s the first generation born after World War II came to maturity. These young adults questioned, and often rejected, many traditional patterns of life, including the nuclear family and accepted sexual behavior and sex roles. The much-heralded sexual revolution may be more evolution than revolution, but it certainly ensured continuing recognition and appreciation of the sexuality of women. The highly publicized work of the American sex researchers William Masters and Virginia Johnson has often been interpreted to mean that women have a greater interest in and potential for sex than men—an almost complete about-face from views held a century ago.[26] Advanced techniques for the avoidance of pregnancy and improved antibiotics supposedly eliminating the danger of venereal infections weakened the force of the two longstanding practical deterrents to sexual intercourse. Dress styles became more informal for both men and women, culminating in the so-called unisex style. This detail in itself is perhaps unimportant, but it is certainly an example of a trend to deny differences between the sexes—at least differences that have any practical significance in terms of life style or possible behavior.

The sudden realization during this period that population control is a worldwide concern focused attention on the virtues of contraception and counteracted some of the traditional societal pressure to "propagate the race." Meanwhile, housekeeping became less and less demanding and less and less satisfying. The idea that the mother must be constantly available to the child was challenged as too narrow an interpretation of Freud's concept, and many women began to realize that they did not necessarily want or need to devote the majority of their energies to their children, nor did the children need this exclusive devotion.

On the political front, the passage by Congress of the Equal Rights Amendment in 1972 stressed further a general trend toward eliminating discrimination. The women's movement is, of course, in no sense monolithic. It comprises a variety of groups, some of which have at least superficially conflicting goals. Nevertheless, they are all in agreement that women should have equal rights with men and should resist accepting a state subservient to men. All agree that inequalities in pay and opportunities for advancement in work should be eliminated. Some women feel that women's independence of men should extend to the sexual sphere, and they may adopt a lesbian way of life. Others see women's independence as meaning their right to approach men openly, to enjoy relationships with them, and to end such relationships on the same basis that men have ended them in the past. Finally, many women feel that affirmative action should be taken to correct imbalances resulting from past inequities.

The women's movement has stressed the right of women to decide if and when they shall have children, pointing out that laws against contraception and abortion were enacted by men, who do not have to suffer the consequences. With great clarity and poignancy, women in and out of the movement have specified a number of conditions which they find repugnant, unjust, and discriminatory. For example, they stress that the general attitude toward women of all classes predisposes them to failure in achieving personal fulfillment and imposes on them the frustrations of stultifying housekeeping chores. They maintain that prevailing sexual and marriage customs exploit and demean women's sexuality, pointing out that marriage is often a bargain in which the wife trades sexual favors in return for her husband's financial support. They feel that women can too often gratify their interests, needs, and aspirations only through their husbands and children, and that women have come increasingly to assume vicarious identities, with the result that their personal self-expression has been stifled.

Thus the 1970s were ushered in by a feminist movement that involved a rather large number of women and enjoyed widespread public attention. Another group of women, however, took a traditional view of women's roles and saw the new feminism as threatening. It is not entirely clear whether these women felt personally threatened or simply wished to dissociate themselves publicly from the feminist group, whose leaders frequently implied that all women "demanded" a particular right. On the whole, however, there has been a widespread raising of consciousness well beyond the immediate reach of feminist activities. Many women who do not consider themselves feminists are becoming increasingly aware of and increasingly vocal about social roles, attitudes, and relationships which they begin to see as condescending, depreciating, or overtly discriminatory, and which reinforce the traditional social structure in subtle ways. This awareness is perhaps keenest among young women in professional, academic, artistic, and intellectual life. But already discussions about the kinds of relationships women have with their boy friends and husbands are beginning to develop among non-college women and to spill over into popular magazines and the advice columns of newspapers.

three

EXPECTATIONS OF WOMEN IN COLLEGE

The college or university frequently, if not always, mirrors the attitudes of the general society toward women and, despite stated goals to the contrary, at times inadvertently reinforces many of these attitudes. As has been pointed out, the idea of equal education for women has become more and more accepted in the United States. At the present time more than 40 per cent of all college undergraduates are women. Women not only are encouraged to enter college but are expected to compete successfully with men in academic pursuits, and in actual fact their academic performance at college is often superior to that of men.

But American society has not also provided opportunities for women to make use of the education they have received. Undergraduate women planning to enter careers find that, while theoretically many are open to women, theory and practice do not always coincide. If one looks at the statistics on women college graduates, one finds that most of those employed are schoolteachers, nurses, and salesclerks. Women represent fewer than 1 per cent of engineers, fewer than 2 per cent of executives, and fewer than 7 per cent of physicians. While these figures have begun to climb upward, there remains a discrepancy between the encouragement of women to do well in college and the opportunities that are offered afterward.[1]

College women who might seek intellectual and professional development face other discouragements. One very visible deterrent is the small number of female faculty members they see in college. Except in women's colleges, women are in a small minority on faculties, and even at some women's colleges the balance is shifting toward men. In the academic year of 1972–1973 there was one female full professor for every ten men who were full professors in American colleges, and when one excludes two-year colleges, the odds are even more heavily in favor of men. At prestigious universities only a handful, about 2 per cent of full professors, 4 or 5 per cent of associate professors, and 10 per cent of assistant professors were women.[2] These ratios naturally convey to women students a sense of limited opportunity. The scarcity of women professors also deprives women students of models for emulation and sources of advice that are available to their male colleagues.

Women's aspirations are also discouraged by the attitudes of male professors and fellow students, who intimate, and sometimes openly state, that "woman's place is in the home." They often imply that a woman should seek a "suitable" job as an interim occupation before she assumes her ultimate role as wife, home-maker, and mother. Or sometimes they expect her to help support her husband through his graduate-school years. It is not unusual for a college woman whose aspirations do not follow this pattern to be asked by her male faculty adviser, "Why does a pretty girl like you want to attend law school?" The implication here is clear: A "normal" female student chooses marriage as her goal, and women plan serious careers only when they are either somewhat "odd" or not pretty enough to attract an offer of marriage. Despite the Women's Liberation movement, this view is still widely held by parents, employers, and even educators. It is also held by many young women themselves. The implicit assumption prevails that this role was ordained by nature and has persisted unchanged through the ages.

Nevertheless, current statistics indicate that 50 per cent of women in the United States, including almost one-third of all mothers of preschool children, hold jobs outside the home. The higher the educational attainment of a woman, the greater the likelihood that she will work outside the home. More than half of all women college graduates are employed, as are 71 per cent of all women with some postgraduate education[3] and 91 per cent of women doctorate holders—almost all on a full-time basis.[4] Many, however, work at job levels lower than one would expect from their educational attainments. And although most women work for economic reasons, participation in the labor force is by no means restricted to low-income groups. In 1971, women worked in 41 per cent of the families in the top 5-per-cent income bracket.[5]

Besides negative attitudes toward careers for women, college women frequently report aspersions on the intellectual capacities of women. Although there are signs that these attitudes are

37

diminishing among male undergraduates, many male students persist in the notion that women do not possess the same objective rationality as men. And studies show a persistent tendency in many, though by no means all women, to "play dumb" in the presence of men so as to conform to this idea. Other studies have shown that a woman's career aspirations are heavily influenced by the attitude of the man she is dating or with whom she has a close relationship. A college woman is frequently distressed to find that her "enlightened" male fellow student believes in sexual equality and the right of women to pursue their own careers only until these concepts affect him directly. The following case vignette illustrates the point:

Nancy had an outstanding academic record in her major, biology. She had considered applying to medical school but decided that she would prefer to teach biology at either college or secondary school. She was encouraged to apply for graduate school by her faculty adviser and was accepted at a prominent Midwestern university.

In her senior year Nancy had become involved with Ben, a fellow senior, who was pre-med. They met initially in a biology class, and he seemed very admiring of her intellectual abilities. Their relationship developed, and both thought in terms of marriage, although they made no definite decision. Ben was accepted at an Eastern medical school, which was his first choice. He was also accepted at a Midwestern school within commuting distance of the university where Nancy was accepted. With very little hesitation, he chose the Eastern school.

The ensuing discussion brought out clearly Ben's view that he was quite amenable to Nancy's working and even having "a career," but that his career was really the crucial one. Consequently, he had no intention of modifying his decision because of Nancy. Nancy was so upset by Ben's attitude and his apparent inflexibility when put to the test that their relationship cooled considerably, and by graduation it was not clear whether they would continue to see each other.

Outside the strictly academic sphere, campus life usually offers a restricted role to women. In coeducational institutions women rarely hold major positions in student government, newspapers, or athletics. In 1970 women constituted only 5 per cent of student-body presidents, 12 per cent of judicial-board chairmen, and 25 per cent of newspaper editors.[6] By contrast, their role as sex objects is emphasized by such ceremonies as that of crowning a Homecoming Queen. Although several colleges have recently abolished this particular ritual, there are students, both male and female, who feel it should be continued.

Until a few years ago much of campus life and the regulations governing it were concerned with the "protection" of women, which usually meant preserving their chastity. Elaborate parietal rules, while ostensibly guarding "morality," nevertheless had the effect of indicating that women were to be thought of in a primarily sexual context.[7] The woman's overprotected and restricted life severely limited her opportunities for growth and development of a healthy autonomy. In contrast, men on campus have always had the freedom and options to allow them to develop self-reliance. The virtual elimination of parietal rules in many colleges across the nation is one indicator that changes are taking place in the attitudes toward, and in the situation of, women. They are beginning to be perceived as capable of making their own decisions about relationships, and of implementing these decisions once they have made them. But there is still a considerable distance to go.

In other respects, colleges have tended to ignore the fact that nearly half of their students are women. Courses in history, sociology, and psychology have neglected to mention the contributions women have made to culture, a neglect that women's studies programs are now remedying in part. College counselors have failed to provide the support that women especially need—for example, information and counseling on birth control, pregnancy, and abortion. To this day such vital services as those of a gynecologist may be either not available on campus at all or available only for a special fee. Advisory services that would specifically orient women toward graduate and professional schools and toward careers have been distinguished either by their absence or by the weakness of their support. Recommendations written for women students applying for jobs or graduate study often stress such qualities as "attractiveness" and "femininity," which are not relevant to the ability to study or to perform on a job.

Many other practices of colleges have worked to the particular detriment of women. Admissions procedures often have been discriminatory. Some institutions have set higher criteria for admission of women than they have for men, creating an imbalance that is injurious to both sexes. Some coeducational institutions admit a smaller number of women than of men. The origin of this last-named practice is not entirely clear, but it seems to be related to the philosophy that having more men than women in a social situation is advantageous to the women—as at those formal dances where a surplus of men (a stagline) is provided so that none of the girls need be wallflowers. The practice strengthens the notion that women are to be considered only in regard to sex, and hinders the process of acquaintance out of which mature relations between the sexes can develop.

In addition, difficulties in re-entering college and in transferring from college to college create problems for married women, because, if their choice of schooling is determined by their husbands, as it often is, they need to be able to move between institutions without loss of credit. The generally accepted idea that the wife follows the husband contributes to these difficulties and frequently places the woman in the uncomfortable position of apparently having to choose between marriage and a career.

In general, our educational institutions tend to shape higher education in relation to the needs of men but not of women. We regard preparation for a career as a process that progresses continuously, and we are suspicious of interruptions. Some Ph.D. programs set a time limit for obtaining the degree which particularly works against those, usually women, who may wish to study less than full time. More help is needed for women graduates who wish to pursue careers but are also faced with household demands. For women who, while their children are young, plan to spend time primarily in the home, continuation of career training or some practice in a career is currently very difficult to arrange. There is a lack of high-level part-time professional jobs, and after taking time off to start a family a woman may well find re-entry into the career mainstream far from easy.

Educational institutions have also failed to meet the challenge of helping women maintain some level of intellectual activity during the peak period of family care. Many women in the "diaper years" have felt a sense of depletion and anxiety about the atrophy of their intellectual abilities which they would not need to experience if our educational system recognized this problem and took such steps toward its solution as providing part-time educational programs or jobs. And few institutions make more than a minimal attempt to offer opportunities to women who wish seriously to pursue further education in their middle years.

Against this background, what are the expectations of today's college women? Sometimes they are confused or, at best, unclear, as the following statements written to gain admission at one college to a course on "The Educated Woman" would indicate:

> Although I've had no formal experience with the study of women, my interest in this seminar is primarily a personal one; because I intend to continue with education, I'll most likely qualify some day as an "educated woman." At present, I have no specific career or "future" plans and would approach this study in light of my own, and my female peers', futures.

> My little thinking about my role as an educated woman before I came to college never had a real testing ground, for I had always lived largely apart from men in my family of six girls and my two schools for girls. When I came to college I was struck by some realization about this role I had (the need to do something because I was a woman, etc.). The novelty of a coed environment and its implications socially and academically have changed my thinking, made it more realistic, more exciting, but often more discouraged.

> I sense many conflicts within myself as to what constitutes a definition of an "educated woman." I read in a recent issue of a new

magazine, *Ms.*, about a study conducted at the University of Michigan which showed that women have a greater tendency not to succeed the higher they pursue their education. Why is this? Does an "educated woman" have to be a superwoman who can reconcile career and family goals so well that neither suffers at the expense of the other? Unfortunately my background in this whole area is very weak, which is why I would like to be in this seminar.

Expectations depend in part on personal background and experience, and in part on the cultural setting in which a woman finds herself, but there are discernible changes at work. Recent surveys of entering college freshmen conducted by the American Council on Education show that, while most college women continue to view marriage and the raising of a family as important personal goals, a steadily increasing number expect to combine family and career.[8] Women are planning to marry later and to have smaller families than they planned even five years ago. Many are beginning to realize that, as a consequence of their desire for smaller families, of the availability of contraception and abortion, and of today's longer life span, they will be devoting a relatively small portion of their adult lives to child-rearing. Many are also influenced by contemporary attitudes which reject the assignment of roles or status on the basis of race, socioeconomic background, or sex, and which put a premium on individualism and autonomy.

In the past, many women who pursued careers remained single or took up careers after their husbands died. Career women who married and raised families were able to do so because they could find and afford adequate domestic help. Today's young women face a different situation. Domestic help is difficult if not impossible to find, and child-care centers are scarce. The graduated income tax means that the second wage-earner (usually the wife) must earn a relatively high salary just to break even. So practical problems for married working women remain serious today even though they differ from problems of the past, and few women have adequate models after whom they can pattern their own lives as they try to cope with newly evolving styles of family life.

Besides the practical problems for women seeking careers, there may be internal barriers that developed in the course of growing up. Differences in the ways boys and girls are trained in society are well known. A recent paper in *American Psychologist* has aptly described the effects of some of them:

> For males, socialization tends to enhance experiential options and to encourage more androgynous sex role definitions since some traditionally feminine concerns (conscientiousness, conservation, interdependency) are emphasized along with the press to renounce negative aspects of the masculine role (opportunism, restlessness, self-centeredness). For women, the socialization process tends to reinforce the nurturant, docile, submissive, and conservative aspects of the traditionally defined female role and discourages personal qualities conventionally defined as masculine: self-assertiveness, achievement orientation, and independence. The sex role definitions and behaviorial options for women, then, are narrowed by the socialization process, whereas, for men, the sex-role definitions and behavioral options are broadened by socialization. The achievement of higher levels of ego functioning for women is more difficult

because individuation involves conflict with our prevailing cultural norms.[9]

Thus women are prepared for the traditional role of wife and mother and barriers are created within them against pursuing a "career" as opposed to "having a job" for an interim or indefinite period. The foundations of these barriers are both conscious and unconscious. Although it is clearly impossible to draw a sharp line between the conscious and the unconscious, it may be helpful to keep these categories in mind.

Two major contributing influences are a woman's expectations of herself and her impression of what others expect of her—or perhaps of a group with which she is identified, such as "college women." These expectations, conscious and unconscious, are often related to each other. A woman may consciously expect to use her talents to their fullest, but unconsciously she may undervalue those talents to such a degree that she feels a serious career is impossible for her. And as for the expectations of others, she may consciously feel that her parents have no particular expectations as to how she will arrange her life, so that theoretically she could pursue a professional career without their disapproval. Unconsciously, however, she may recognize that her mother prides herself on her full-time homemaking, and in consequence she may fear that any other choice will be unacceptable to her parents.

In more general terms, a young girl's formation of her own identity is strongly influenced by her idea of what it means to be a woman. And this idea itself is influenced by family values, the attitudes of society, and personal experiences, all of which interact with the girl's own physical and psychological attributes.

Once a girl has developed her identity (or self-image), she must measure it against her own view of the qualities required to follow a particular life path successfully and of what the implications are. If she feels that to be successful in business one must be sharp, aggressive, and willing to sacrifice one's "personal" life, this feeling may clash with her sense of her own abilities and inclinations, or, more complexly, with her concept of the behavior appropriate to a woman.

Similar considerations can obviously affect the boy's choice of a career, but, as the paper just cited points out, his vision of what is required of him to be a business success is much more likely to agree with what society expects of him as a male.[10] The woman feels faced with the dilemma of either abandoning the idea of the career or radically changing her idea of herself, which may be very difficult to do and may not seem worth doing.

Also a part of this problem is the woman's view of her relationship to men and how it may be affected by her choice of career. Obviously, she has more than her self-image to deal with here. If she becomes involved more than once with men who are unwilling to be flexible toward her career plans and who end the relationships, she will inevitably begin to ponder the difficulties her career choice has created for her personal life. If there is any uncertainty in her mind (and in what college student is there not uncertainty?), she may wonder whether the end is worth the losses along the way. She may need considerable faith and courage to forge ahead, either trusting that eventually a relationship with a man can be worked out or running the risk that she will never have such a relationship.

One could say that a man is in a similar position, but two

prevalent attitudes make a critical difference. First, most people consider that a man is responsible for providing his family's support (this is actually the legal fact). For him, embarking on a career is seen as an approved and even necessary step toward establishing a permanent relationship with a woman. Second is the corollary view that the woman does not need to earn a living because the man will provide for her. She may even be seen as deliberately complicating her life by considering a career.

In the area of intelligence, many inaccurate ideas have been accepted unquestioningly by young women and their male friends. One of these is the notion that intelligence and logical thinking are "biologically" masculine attributes and that a woman has a built-in handicap in any field in which these are important. Even when a young woman is aware that her own intelligence is equivalent to that of the men she knows, she may worry that showing her intelligence will threaten her relationships with them. Although neither attitude may be clearly perceived by the woman on a conscious level, both feelings may join to create a very real internal obstacle to her choice of a serious career. Or because she accepts the conventional view that the wife should not outperform the husband, a woman student may conclude that professional success will reduce the available pool of eligible men for her to choose from.

Closely related to a male-female relationship is the issue of motherhood and child-rearing. The ability to have children is inevitably part of the concept of being a woman. Most girls have some anticipation of becoming mothers. Their attitude toward motherhood is probably most deeply influenced by their own childhood experiences or by distorted memories of these experi-

47

ences. It may also be affected by popular views of child-rearing, particularly those expressed by potential husbands. If the woman herself has some feeling that motherhood should be a full-time occupation at least during the child's preschool years, this feeling may turn her away from a career requiring consistent endeavor. Or she may feel that commitment to a career at a time when motherhood is not a real possibility will only cause severe conflict when she does marry. In short, she may fear that the difficulties of combining a career with marriage and family are so great that she must make a choice. Rather than choose a career while in college and find out whether marriage and children can be integrated with it when the time comes, she may choose marriage and family and, if they are not immediately attainable, occupy herself with an interim job. The following comment by a woman with a graduate degree, made in answer to the question in a survey of women with advanced degrees, "Do you feel that you confronted special problems in employment or education because you are a woman?" illustrates several of these points.

I have never encountered any discrimination on account of sex, unless possibly favorable discrimination. The special problems I have had come not from being a woman, but from being a married woman. I have had to change jobs twice because of moves my husband made, one of which was necessary and one clearly beneficial to him. This is a problem both partners would be likely to have to face in any marriage in which both are committed to careers. In both job changes, I found a position suitable to my qualifications; both my husband and I held out for that. Both changes were probably, on balance, good for me. Nevertheless, this is a special problem that someone who is not married, or someone whose career is clearly identified as the dominant one (in our society, usually still the husband), need not face.

The other two problems I have had to deal with have come from being a woman who decided to have children as well as a career. The practical as well as the emotional strain of implementing that decision is great. Pregnancy and recovery create a problem with regard to work that, however it is solved, is obviously a problem no man has to deal with. Once the existence of children is taken care of, one's life (and one's husband's) depends upon the quality of child care available. These are not exactly problems in employment, but they are closely connected with employment; either they affect work, or work affects them.

Needless to say, if I had married before finishing my education, that, too, might have been influenced. As it was, my commitment to my studies probably influenced me to marry later than many girls in our society.

Another influence on a woman's internal motivation is the real difficulty facing women in many fields. This situation may make a woman depressed or apathetic—"It's not worth the fight," or, "Why try, when even men are having trouble getting jobs?" A man cannot so easily accede to this feeling because he is expected to pursue a career so that he will be able to support a family. (Recently, however, some men have begun "dropping out," perhaps partly because of this same feeling.) For the woman, however, there is an alternative that is not only acceptable but also promises certain satisfactions (whether they materialize or not) in the form of companionship, motherhood, and financial support.

Of course there are always a few women who react in the opposite way, women who, if told that a given field is virtually closed to them, consider it a challenge and deliberately enter it. In general, however, this reaction is not typical for women, and even a woman like this may be blocked by her concept of what is appropriate behavior for a woman.

In the long run everyone, male or female, attempts to chart a life course calculated, as far as can be predicted, to provide the greatest satisfaction. But rarely do one's unconscious and conscious feelings all mesh and point unequivocally in one direction; more often they in some measure conflict. When reconciliation of conflicting feelings is not possible, a choice must be made, and then external factors may determine this choice by supporting or canceling out one or another of the contradictory internal elements. It is the complex interplay of internal feelings and external realities that is in the end crucial. The following answer to a question about career difficulties illustrates this interplay:

The worst problem I had to overcome was within myself, i.e., the feeling that I needn't be serious about graduate school and a career because I was going to get married and be supported by my husband. Almost every female academic I know has faced or is facing this problem in some guise.

Putting aside this emotional problem, I faced very real discrimination when I went looking for a job (late 1968 to early 1969). Several potential employers told me at our convention that they were looking for someone, but would not consider a woman, even though my credentials were excellent. When I took the job at [X University] I was hired as a Lecturer, even though I had my Ph.D., and in addition, I was paid less than three men also hired that year, none of whom had completed the doctorate.

The emphasis on career in the foregoing discussion should not obscure the fact that for many women the job of wife and mother provides a complete and fulfilling life. The pursuit of a career or combined marriage and career must not be set up as a standard against which all college women should measure themselves: these alternatives have been stressed, rather than the homemaker role, because many influences in our culture today press women into the latter position.

four

THE FEMININE-MASCULINE AXIS

As the previous discussion indicates, there are biological, developmental, and sociocultural factors that define the similarities and differences between men and women. These are important because such clichés as "It's a woman's nature" or "It's characteristically masculine" are used to justify certain traditions and patterns. The reasons for these views need to be examined.

The traditional view is that male and female roles are determined by "nature," which is defined to mean the different biological and psychological characteristics of the male and the female. The new view is that many of these characteristics are in reality a result of social conditioning, and those which are not need not, in most instances, determine specific roles. The thrust of this new view is toward equality of opportunity for both sexes, the implication being that if this were to be achieved the sexes would be represented equally in most roles—suggesting that men and women are generally similar in their capabilities. This assumption has been questioned by those who believe that males and females constitutionally have bodies, emotional patterns, and interests which are characteristic of their sex and make them fit or unfit for certain tasks. Although there are research data to support both views, they are often cited for emotional or political purposes, or because of unconscious attitudes, rather than as objective judgments.

The terms *masculinity* and *femininity* sum up many of the facts known and many of the feelings people have about the sexes. A definition of these terms is essential, to bring some order to the confusion surrounding them, and to clarify what people mean when they speak of a person's self-fulfillment "as a woman" or "as a man."

The question then arises: Are there any specific experiences that a female or a male must have to achieve fulfillment, or do these experiences differ for every individual, whether male or female? Knowledge of this subject is incomplete, but it is important to examine what is known, to separate biological from cultural factors, and to identify, where possible, some of the psychological and social elements that affect the concepts of male and female, masculine and feminine.

Definitions of Sex and Gender

One of the great problems in discussing men and women, their roles and relationships, is the confusion and the lack of precision in terminology. Such terms as *male* and *female* or *masculine* and *feminine* are used loosely without specification as to whether one is referring to a biological attribute, cultural stereotype, physiological characteristic, or some second-rank association of trait with sex—for example, associating the trait of aggressiveness with the male. One might assume that the terms *male* and *female* are quite clear, but recent research on anomalies in the newborn has underlined difficulties, in certain cases, even in the assignment of sex—that is, determining whether an individual is male or female.

Terms such as *sexual identity* and *gender identity* are also used to describe without clear differentiation the individual's internal self-image as a male or female or the preferred mode of sexual behavior as heterosexual or homosexual. Finally, the terms *sex role* and *gender role* seem to suggest a description of the person's function in a social context as a male or a female, but, given the fact that male and female roles differ greatly from culture to culture and even from group to group within a culture, it is difficult to ascertain the true meaning of the terms unless one also defines the social context.

Because these imprecise definitions are frequently used in ignorant and/or partisan fashion, and arguments are based on their assigned meanings, it is particularly important to define them here as clearly as possible and to adhere to these definitions throughout.

The dictionary is of relatively little help, but it does define *sex* as "One of the two divisions of organisms formed on the distinction of male and female." [1] American pediatrician and sex researcher John Money has pointed out, however, that even this division is not easily defined in a scientific sense. [2] He cites five biological factors that are involved: (1) nuclear sex, as demonstrated by chromosome pattern; (2) gonadal sex, shown by the presence of testes or ovaries; (3) hormonal sex, identified by the pattern of hormonal productions; (4) internal accessory structures, uterus or prostate; and (5) external genital morphology, penis and testes, or vagina. In most individuals all five factors are consonant, and assignment of sex is based on external genital morphology. When a baby is born, the genitals are inspected and the child is designated a girl or a boy. When external genital morphology is ambiguous, as it sometimes is, suggesting lack of consonance in the five factors, other factors must be considered. It has become quite clear, however, that *the sex that is assigned and the rearing—that is, how the parents define and respond to the child's sex—are the most important influences in determining the individual's later sense of being male or female.*

Gender is defined by the dictionary mainly in reference to grammar—that is, those words which are of masculine or feminine gender in certain languages.[3] John Money and Anke Ehrhardt define gender identity and gender role as follows:

Gender identity: The sameness, unity, and persistence of one's individuality as male, female, or ambivalent, in greater or lesser degree, especially as it is experienced in self-awareness and behavior; gender identity is the private experience of gender role, and gender role is the public expression of gender identity.

Gender role: Everything that a person says and does, to indicate to others or to the self the degree that one is either male, or female, or ambivalent; it includes but is not restricted to sexual arousal and response; gender role is the public expression of gender identity, and gender identity is the private experience of gender role.[4]

55

Sexual orientation usually refers to the preferred adult sexual behavior of the individual as heterosexual, homosexual, or bisexual and is here so used in preference to the more ambiguous term *sexual identity*.

BIOLOGICAL ASPECTS OF MALE AND FEMALE

Generally speaking, most animal species are divided into two subclasses, males and females, each having characteristic anatomical features, patterns of physiological response, and specific ways of relating to each other. One way of relating which embraces all three sets of characteristics is sexual and is essential for reproduction. This holds true for human beings, who display all three characteristics but in addition may have certain culturally imposed differences, such as style of dress, mode of grooming, or life tasks, also assigned on the basis of sex. The terms *masculine* and *feminine* are adjectives used to denote characteristics associated with either males or females. These characteristics may be based on biological, physiological, psychological, or behavioral attributes, some of which may be inherited and some learned, while many result from the interaction between inheritance and learning.

Among the most noteworthy characteristics of the human species are a capacity for considerable plasticity and an ability to adapt in many diverse ways. An example is the ability, in appropriate circumstances, to interchange almost totally behavior generally considered masculine with that considered feminine. Such is the enormous capacity of the human psyche for adaptation that it seems as though almost the entire range of behavioral characteristics can be developed by a member of either sex. Cross-cultural studies indicate that human cultures vary widely in the traits and activities specifically considered masculine or feminine. In fact, the same trait is often assigned to one sex by one culture and to the opposite sex by another.[5] For example, in many cultures heavy physical work is assigned to women, whereas in our culture it is more often thought of as a male activity.

Males and females go through stages in their development both biologically and psychologically, so that their attributes change over a period of time. A particularly important change biologically, physiologically, and psychologically occurs at puberty, when hormonal patterns alter, secondary sex characteristics appear, and both males and females become biologically ready for their respective roles in reproduction. At this point the biological differences between males and females become more sharply marked, and certain patterns of sexual response are to be found in both males and females—for example, they are aroused by each other. However, some adults are aroused by individuals of the same sex, indicating that factors can intervene to prevent development of the usual response. Because sexual behavior is one sphere in which males and females play clearly different roles, it of course plays a large part in defining concepts of masculinity and femininity.

Even this connection, however, has become remarkably complex as a result of increasing knowledge. The American psychiatrist Warren Gadpaille, in an excellent review article, mentions the many variables which must be considered and outlines areas of current knowledge as well as of ignorance.[6] His review discusses a large amount of animal experimentation designed to isolate central-nervous-system and hormonal factors in sexual behavior, advances in the understanding of human sexual behavior made through the study of various pathological human conditions involving chromosomal or hormonal anomalies, and careful studies of developmental influences on gender identity. The correlations between these studies are complex and somewhat speculative, but a summary of his conclusions may be useful.

Experiments have determined that in rats there is a critical fetal period during which the presence of the male hormone androgen causes the development of normal male genitalia, the organization of the brain in such a way that a male pattern of hormonal release is established, and, in the adult rat, male sexual behavior in response to a female. The absence of androgen at the critical fetal period results in female genitalia, female hormonal release patterns, and female sex response in *all* rats, regardless of whether they are of male or female genotype (chromosomal pattern).

Studies on primates are less advanced but so far have tended to give similar results. In addition, observation has revealed that primates do not display adult sexual behavior unless the individuals have had adequate mothering, social contact with their peers, and childhood sex play. This fact suggests the increasing importance to sexual behavior of the cerebral cortex and of socialization processes as one approaches the human level in the phylogenetic scale. Although research which requires laboratory intervention during gestation obviously cannot be conducted with human subjects, certain "natural" developmental anomalies have been observed which mimic some of those found in laboratory experimental conditions and bear out many of the findings from animal research.

Gadpaille draws several conclusions from these data. The first is that female morphology is basic, regardless of genotype, and males develop only when androgen is present in appropriate quantity during a critical fetal period. This androgen, when present, has two effects: It governs the development of normal male genitalia, and it organizes a part of the brain in a particular (masculine) way so that it will later regulate hormonal output in the normal male (acyclic) manner. Without androgen, female genitalia will develop (although female genotype is necessary for procreative functioning), and the relevant part of the brain will be organized to release hormones in the female (cyclic) manner. Gadpaille believes that this part of the brain also affects later sexual response. He recognizes, however, that the higher the species in the phylogenetic scale, the more crucial is socializing in determining the outcome, and that at the human level rearing can dominate all other factors in deciding the individual's self-concept of gender and adult sexual response.

Gadpaille also cites a statistical study that distinguished males from females by a series of criteria, including energy level, toy and sports preferences, and basis for erotic arousal. Although he recognizes the possibility that some of these distinctions may be culturally determined, he feels that others are clearly independent of cultural influence, and he explains these differences as arising from differences in brain organization caused by the presence or absence of androgen in the critical fetal period. "It seems likely," he says, "that there are definable differences in masculine and feminine behavior, attitudes, and preferences that are traceable to the simple biological fact of being male or female (assuming biologically normal development) and that all such differences are not purely cultural artifacts." [7] On the other hand, he recognizes that, for any individual, the sex assigned and the rearing (whether the child is brought up as a boy or a girl) can outweigh all other factors.

It should be noted that other observers take issue with Gadpaille's conclusions, but his thinking is an indication of current attempts in research to illuminate a controversial subject. [8]

Although gender identity is almost always determined by the sex of assignment and the rearing, what determines the gender role and the adult sex response is more problematic—as the controversy started by Gadpaille's conclusions illustrates—but clearly it must be discussed in considering the roles of women and men. Biological, environmental, sociological, and moral issues continually and variably complicate the formation of our psychological concepts. In understanding concepts of masculinity and femininity, should our emphasis be upon the perceived differences or upon the actual and anticipated similarities in function, personality, and even appearance? The current strivings for sex equality carry with them a certain tendency toward similarity between the sexes—a single life style for both males and females, a sameness of function except where this is anatomically unrealizable in the most restricted sense. This point of view and the proposals which accompany it are based on the assumptions that males and females are essentially the same and when they are not the same, emotionally and behaviorally, social learning is the cause, and social learning—theoretically, at least—is alterable, so that the two sexes can be *made* equal and similar.

So there are two opposing views current today. One view is that there are indeed innate biophysiological differences between the sexes, some of which may be modified by social conditioning, but only through specific efforts; the other view contends that almost all emotional and behavioral differences are a product of socialization. Proponents of the two views may also differ significantly on the benefits of minimizing the differences. Somewhere between these two propositions one finds the psychoanalytic view that the anatomical structure of each sex leads inevitably to a certain kind of experience for that sex, more of an emotional than of an intellectual nature, and that this experience, interwoven with social learning, contributes in a major way to personality development, including self-concept, and thus to behavioral differences between the sexes. Freud's explanation, which embodies the whole theory of psychosexual development, was more complex than either the biological or the socialization view, but it now appears to be in part a reflection of the patterns of thought prevalent in his time. For example, in associating a passive attitude with the female's receptivity in the act of conception, he was relating biological function to psychological characteristic. Evidence from cross-cultural studies and later psychoanalytic observations have caused revision of many of Freud's early notions, yet seem to confirm the existence of some more or less sex-related traits, such as aggressiveness in the male or mothering in the female, that appear to be independent of cultural patterns of the societies in which they are found. Recent sex research has also questioned some of Freud's assumptions, but some scientists feel that it has not wholly disproved the fundamental tenets of Freud's theory.[9]

Development in Childhood

Even though gender identity is established early in life, experiences as the child grows are highly influential in communicating the meaning of being male or female, in determining the eventual concept of the gender role, in forming adult patterns of personal relationships, and in sexual orientation and behavior. How do people come to define *for themselves* what is masculine or feminine in the course of their own development, and how does this self-concept affect their adult sexual response?

Because children develop by reacting to a series of human relationships, the concepts of self and of the ideal self bear the stamp of these relationships. At birth the infant requires a dependable caretaker in order to survive. This first essential relationship profoundly influences the baby's psychological potentials. Its effect on the child's innate capacities is so profound that it is difficult to separate the "biological" development from the "psychological" or environmental influences. Actually, development is psychobiological, and biology and psychology proceed together.

The caretaking person may in fact be the child's biological mother, but this person may also be the father, another relative, a nurse, or an older sibling; or in fact several individuals may share the caretaking functions. The word *mother* is used here for the person who occupies the chief caretaking role for the child. (Although the feminine gender is used in the discussion that follows, it should be understood that the gender of the caretaking person is probably not important in the first months of life.)

Separation and closeness. The mother's conception of herself in relation to her child influences her behavior with the child and, in consequence, the child's self-concept. If the mother unconsciously thinks of her child as merely an extension of herself, the child may perceive himself or herself as only an extension of the mother. If the mother thinks of the child only in terms of the child's demands upon her, she will influence the child in the direction of dependency; conversely, if the mother encourages the child's participation in self-care, the child will be influenced to value an inner potential for initiative. Simultaneously, the child is learning about the boundaries between himself or herself and the mother.

At first the child exists in a symbiotic relationship with the mother, which is essential for survival; the experiencing of *separateness*, however, is necessary for the child's continued development. Gradually self is differentiated from nonself, and then comes the concept of a separate self, which relates to the mother as another, separate person. Ideally, the mother is able to respond to the child's needs for both closeness and distance. Distance provides the opportunity for *manageable experiences of separation* from the mother—for example, the toddler explores situations away from the mother and returns to her from time to time.[10] Such experiences are essential for developing capacities for both separateness and closeness in the maturing individual.

The child's image of the mother does not correspond exactly to the reality of the mother but is related to the child's perceptual capacities and needs at various stages of development. For example, children may perceive the mother principally in terms of her capacity to diminish or increase their feelings of tension. Thus, when the child is frustrated and overwhelmed by internal feelings and can be immediately reassured and satisfied by the mother's ministrations, the child may think of the mother as quite powerful and may also view these caretaking functions as the only functions the mother has.

For both boys and girls these early experiences with the mother provide a basis for their attitudes about women in later life. If *the mother* feels she has value only as a caretaker, she may reinforce the child's early images of her in these terms. The child's feelings may become unconscious and in adult life may cause the individual to view women exclusively as providers of gratification and relievers of distress, and thus to have certain expectations about what is "reasonable" in a close relationship. The following case vignette involving a parent-child relationship is illustrative:

> Mrs. X, in analysis, discussed her difficulty in getting her six-year-old son to bed. In order for her to feel like a "good mother," it was necessary that her son not be in conflict with her and agree that *he* also wished to go to bed. Naturally, he did not always feel this way. She would then engage in a long power struggle and debate, often ending in an explosive, punitive outburst on her part which settled the matter but left her feeling "bad" and deserving punishment from the child. This would set the stage for the next cycle, when she again would redouble her efforts to be a "good mother."
>
> Mrs. X's own mother had difficulty in being direct about her own needs when they conflicted with her daughter's. She relived with her own child her own internalization of the mother-child relationship. To part of her, a "good mother" was only a providing mother with no needs of her own. When conflict arose in her relationship with her child she felt either she had become a "bad mother" or else the

child was "bad" for wanting something she did not wish to give. She could only set limits for the child in the context of feeling like a "bad mother." Similarly, she could not feel like a "good mother" if she recognized that it was her fatigue which in part determined her child's bedtime.

Body image and self-concept. From experiences with his or her own body, the child forms a *body image*. This is the beginning of the self-concept.[11] Feelings about the body can have an important effect. Does the child think of it as a source of pleasure? How do those around him react to the child's body and biological functions? For example, if the child feels that a particular bodily activity is in danger of being taken over by others, this activity may be viewed in terms of a power struggle. In this way, eating can come to be thought of as belonging outside of the self and subject to regulation for the benefit of others, as can urination and defecation. Failure to allow the child to participate in decisions about these functions may give him a rather one-sided view of them. If such patterns persist, the child may grow up to feel that all personal relationships are matters of domination, submission, and power. If the child and the parents can handle these activities together, the chances are that the child's relationships in later life will be more collaborative. Unconscious residues of these early experiences may affect adult sexual relationships, which involve both bodily activity and response to another person.

Parental values. Children's feelings about their bodies and themselves also reflect the nature of the family structure and the family's values. In some families only qualities that are endowed with or represent "maleness" are valued. It is not surprising that a male child in such a family tends to consider his penis one of the most important parts of his body, and he may also feel that physical strength, courage, and the ability to fight (or whatever the family designates as masculine) are essential qualities. A female child in such a family may feel that the absence of a penis and of qualities of strength and courage represents a grave liability for her in achieving a sense of value as a person (this attitude is often referred to in psychoanalytic literature as *penis envy*).[12] Similarly, a boy may feel threatened by a lack of these traits, imagined or real, or by any signs of "femaleness" in himself. The girl may overvalue any attribute of hers, such as her clitoris or her physical strength, that may represent for her a form of "maleness"; she may also undervalue parts of her personality or her body, such as her vagina, which represent "femaleness" to her.

On the other hand, if it seems to the child that the mother powerfully dominates the father, "femaleness" may be overvalued. A male child in such a family may be fearful of his own maleness and feel that his penis or any representation of his father in himself is a liability. A female child may, in response to her mother's contempt for maleness, depreciate qualities in herself or others which she identifies as being connected with her father. To sum up, although the process of internalization—that is, incorporating outside attitudes into the self-concept—is part of development for everyone, precisely what gets internalized may vary greatly for particular children even within the same family, depending on the place of each in the family and on the child's perception of the parents.[13]

Identification. The development of the self-concept is also profoundly influenced by the process of identification. The first identification for both girls and boys is with the mother, and it is important for learning as well as essential for psychological growth. In the girl's development, this primary identification with her mother is consonant with a female gender identity. However, as a basis for future heterosexual orientation, she must shift some of her initial attachment from her mother to her father.

For the boy, an attachment to his mother is consistent with his presumed future sexual orientation but not with gender identity, so that he must achieve some distance from his initial identification with his mother, form an attachment to his father, and shift to a principal identification with his father.[14]

It is much easier for a boy to identify with his father if the mother values the father and his male qualities. The boy, through his identification with his mother's attitudes, can then value his own masculinity. Similarly the girl is assisted in her attachment to her father by identifying with her mother's interest in him. The emotional availability of the father is important for the boy to assist his identification as a male, and for the girl in her self-definition as a female. Both boys and girls to some extent internalize both parents' views of femininity and masculinity.

Because the child has attachments to both parents and at times wishes to have an exclusive arrangement with one, the child will also feel varying degrees of competition and rivalry with the parent of the same sex (referred to as Oedipal feelings). This inevitable rivalry, however, is not restricted only to the parent of the same sex. The resolution of these conflicting feelings about parents is an important determinant of the child's emerging personality and sexual development. In some families the chief

67

rival is the mother for the boy or the father for the girl. In other situations the absence, or the perceived ineffectuality, of the parent of the same sex may mean that the child has no experience with competition and consequently aggrandizes his or her self-worth. Because no actual test or competition ever takes place, the child develops a paradoxical sense of special superiority and at the same time a conviction of vulnerability.

The child is not only envious of, but is also relieved and supported in his or her growth by a strong attachment between the parents. It makes the development of friendships with other children easier and frees the child's energy for growth as an autonomous person. The child is relieved to know that, however much he or she wishes it, there will never actually have to be a final confrontation with one parent in a life-and-death battle for the other. To a degree, of course, the boy needs his mother to respond to his maleness just as the girl needs her father to respond to her femaleness.[15] This response gives each one the confidence to attract a sexual partner later on. The absence of such responsiveness on the part of the parent, or an exaggerated response, can pose problems for the child.

Anxieties and conflicts. Between the ages of three and five, the child may have important feelings about the penis and the qualities it symbolizes. When these feelings persist into adulthood, problems arise. The adult male may compare himself to a "phallic ideal" and expect himself to be an aggressive, hard-driving Superman (unconsciously thinking of the qualities of an erect penis). Feelings that do not fit this ideal, such as tenderness and compassion, may be felt as threats and lower his self-esteem or give him a sense of emasculation. Correspondingly, the female may compare herself with a related ideal which is oriented toward the absence of phallic qualities (being soft, yielding, unassertive). This ideal leaves her vulnerable to the feeling that self-interest, initiative, and competence are masculine qualities which she should not develop for fear of being "unfeminine."

At another extreme, the man may have difficulty exerting his capacity for self-assertion and strength *because* he unconsciously associates these qualities with masculinity and has fears of retaliation (referred to as *castration anxiety*). Similarly for the woman, receptive or tender feelings may also seem threatening to her *because* they are "feminine." In other words, some men and some women may experience anxiety about both "feminine" and "masculine" qualities in themselves, depending on how these qualities have been defined for them in early life. The following case illustrates difficulties arising from failure to resolve such conflicts:

Mr. Y, a thirty-two-year-old very successful and depressed lawyer in analysis, responded to helpful comments from the analyst with self-criticism and feelings of inadequacy. He felt himself inferior in relation to the analyst's insights, and he attributed a power to the analyst which was in part a replica of his feelings about his father, whom he also endowed with an almost magical sense of potency. He measured himself against this ideal, to which he equated the analyst, and felt impotent when he experienced the analyst as more capable than himself.

At the same time, Mr. Y viewed sensitivity and awareness as feminine, belonging to the women in his family. For him, anything other than activity was viewed as feminine, so he felt threatened by his potential for self-awareness. For varying reasons, he felt anxious when he was helped by the analyst in the analysis. It threatened his sense of masculinity to be helped and to be reminded that he was not his omnipotent ideal. He projected onto the analyst both an aspect of himself which he regarded as feminine and at the same time his supermasculine ideal. The analysis enabled him to develop a different ideal for himself which could encompass and also value qualities of sensitivity and self-awareness that might conventionally be interpreted as feminine, as well as activity and mastery.

A further contribution to the sense of oneself as an adult, particularly as a sexual person, is made by the child's perception of the parents' relationship, for from this is absorbed what it is to be a wife or a husband. Even children who consciously reject their parents as models are nevertheless influenced by exposure to them, for the experience is unconsciously made part of them. It contributes to the child's ideal self-concept—that is, the sense of how one *ought* or *ought not* to be as a spouse.[16] The parents' day-to-day communication reveals some of their own concepts of maleness and femaleness, and by constantly observing them, the child surmises something about the essence of their relationship, including some notions about their sexual life, whether it is actually witnessed or not. The child's image of the intimate parental relationship may portray it as intrusive, aggressive, cooperative, assaultive, tender, or whatever, depending on the particular relationship between the parents and how the child feels about it. Often such childhood imagery is lived out in intimate relationships and sexual experiences in later life, as the following case vignette illustrates:

Mrs. Z, a young woman who consciously sought a more gratifying and egalitarian sexual partnership, nonetheless reported in her treatment that she "collaborated" in assaultive rapelike sexual attacks by her husband. Her childhood was filled with accounts by her mother of her father's brutishness, and she identified with her mother's view of her father. She conceived of her parents' sexual experiences as ones in which her father intrusively and brutally attacked her mother.

Without being aware of it, Mrs. Z was reliving this conception of her parents' relationship in her marriage and unwittingly encouraging her husband to act out this imagery with her, although it conflicted with her consciously held concepts of what she wanted.

The child is, of course, also subject to influences outside the home, and of course absorbs concepts from the society, not only about how to be a person but also about how to be a boy or a girl. In children's experience with others outside the home, they may become aware of different models for being a person and also different definitions of masculinity and femininity. These models influence the child's ideal self-concept, which in turn will affect self-esteem, according to how far, in the child's own opinion, he or she lives up to this ideal.

DEVELOPMENT IN ADOLESCENCE

With the onset of puberty, the changes associated with the development of secondary sexual characteristics take place and must be integrated with the existing self-concept, ideas of sexuality, and impressions about gender roles from earlier developmental phases. For some children the emergence of bodily

71

changes representing further self-definition as a sexual person may evoke considerable anxiety, while for others such changes may be welcome and nonthreatening. The onset of menstruation in girls and the development of the capacity for ejaculation in boys are not only physiological changes; they also have psychological correlates, and the meaning assigned to each is influenced by the individual's previous self-concept. A girl who has absorbed a depreciating view of women or of herself may regard menstruation as the expression of her "badness," and her menstrual fluid as visible evidence of "bad stuff" in her. In contrast, a girl with a more favorable view of women may view menstruation as a step toward the status of a grown woman and so respond positively. Bodily configurations such as size of breasts or penis, shape of hips, amount of fat, and so on assume importance in relation to the symbolic meaning which the adolescent assigns to these body parts. Self-worth tends to be linked to these bodily changes, the impact of which varies, depending on the adolescent's ideal.

In adolescence the principal task of development centers on efforts to consolidate a mature sense of personal identity, and considerable experimenting with a variety of consciously chosen self-concepts may precede such consolidation. These efforts may conflict with unconscious feelings left over from childhood. Old concepts of selfhood and identity are not and cannot be discarded simply by choosing a new way of defining oneself. The outcome of these identity struggles during adolescence does not always conform to some cultural ideal. Rather, as people do in every phase of development, adolescents attempt to find some way of integrating different aspects of themselves with alternative models perceived in the environment. In each phase of development certain critical conflicts arise, the outcome of which will affect the next phase, and in every subsequent phase there is some overlap and reworking of what has gone before. Change itself may provoke anxiety, but many psychiatrists believe that some conflict and disturbance are part of healthy development and actually lead to further growth.

In summary, the vitally important feeling of self-worth is dependent on the extent to which one's self-concept approximates the ideal self. Each stage of development, from infancy throughout the life cycle, makes important contributions to the formation of the self-image.

SEXUAL ORIENTATION, BEHAVIOR, AND GENDER ROLE

Male and female gender roles are often seen as representing opposing traits, so that a definition of one implies a definition of the other. These traits are frequently related to sexual behavior. Because the one unequivocal event involving the anatomical and physiological differences between a male and a female is the sexual act of reproduction, sexual behavior in its various aspects has at times been used to define the quintessential characteristics of "maleness" and "femaleness." Qualities necessary to perform the sexual act, such as the male's penetration and thrust or the female's receptiveness, have been generalized and applied to "masculine" or "feminine" behavior in all sorts of situations.

73

Thus, the individual's sexual response and orientation have been viewed as closely related to concepts of masculinity and femininity.

Recent research has challenged the validity of such definitions. However, because it is difficult for most people to separate the gender role from the sexual function, the association remains psychologically important.

As has already been noted, recent studies of animal development have stressed the effect of early biological and social conditions on adult sexual response. Sexual behavior in human beings, however, is probably the most difficult aspect of male and female behavior to document. Restrictions on experiments involving human subjects limit some sources of data. Case histories and subjective impressions or recollections, which are prominent sources of data, are open to the usual criticisms regarding their reliability and representative character. The extensive experimental work of recent years has added vast and rich material, but questions still arise owing to the artificiality of laboratory conditions and the nature of the sampling (which is largely dependent on volunteer subjects).

Researchers have catalogued traits, both specific and general, which have traditionally been ascribed to each gender, and have found statistical differences. These include differences in aggressiveness, in interests ("inner space" or "outer space"), in physical durability, in special aptitudes (intuitive or analytical), in concern with predictability of the environment ("preservers" or "experimenters"), in sensory perception, and in rate of mental and physical maturation. It is not clear, however, whether these differences are rooted in biology or in social conditioning. Alfred

Kinsey, the well-known American zoologist and sex researcher, observed that males appear to be more readily conditioned by sexual experience than females, and more prone to establish associative links between sexual and nonsexual stimuli.[17] In the last decade the work of Masters and Johnson has concentrated an enormous amount of attention on the orgasm.[18] One of the important possibilities they inferred was that females, in contrast to males, may be naturally multiorgasmic. Overall, however, these investigators have emphasized the remarkable physiological *similarities* between male and female sexual response.

During intrauterine life the rudimentary genitalia in female and male embryos gradually evolve into ovary and testes, clitoris and penis. It does not seem far-fetched to assume that the experience of the boy, whose organs are highly visible and palpable, must differ from that of the girl, who discovers her own genitals more gradually by sensation and exploration. These anatomical differences represent the most highly specific biological distinctions between the sexes until puberty, when patterns of sexual hormone production begin to vary. It is probable that hormones affect sexual responsiveness as well as secondary sex characteristics. The specific effects of the individual hormones are complex, but the pattern of hormonal activity may exert different pressures on the behavior of boys and girls in addition to affecting their physical development.

Another important differentiating biological factor is the male accumulation of seminal fluid, which is discharged periodically, through active efforts of the male—by masturbation, intercourse, and so forth—or, in the absence of action, by spontaneous nocturnal emission. Secretions are a product of female sexual arousal, but they are very different from seminal fluid. The mechanism of sexual desire is still poorly understood,[19] but the demand for orgasms may be physiologically more pressing for males early in adolescence (males have been observed to engage in masturbation more frequently than females), whereas females may often have to learn to have orgasms—but it is also possible that underlying biological need has been inhibited in the female by developmental influences and simply needs to be released. One finding that may support this possibility is that males reach a peak of orgasmic activity about a decade earlier than do females.

There is at present, however, no method of determining whether this difference is due to biological or social factors. One might speculate that if the difference is primarily a matter of social conditioning, current changes in attitudes toward sexuality may lead to a shift, but it is too soon to have amassed sufficient data. On the other hand, evidence that the difference is essentially biological would tend to confirm the theory that the role of pursuer, aggressor, and initiator is in fact related to being male. Physiologists and biochemists may well be able to add significantly to this sketch of obvious biological differences between the sexes, and indeed their findings may some day provide the essential data required for a better understanding of sexuality and its place in personality development. Meanwhile, many beliefs about female sexuality continue to find currency.

These are simply accepted generalizations based on some evidence and some theory. One important belief is that there is a pattern of feminine qualities that results in a tendency to look inward. The American psychoanalyst Erik Erikson introduced the concept of "inner space," which is based on the idea of the uterus, the "inner space" in which the child grows during gestation.[20] Another belief is that, in regard to sexual activity, the woman takes a greater interest in a full relationship with another person than in the specific act of intercourse. This implies that sexual expression is more dependent in females than in males on an experience of love or a romantic illusion about love. Related to this is the seeming diffusion of sexual feelings in the female to embrace the total sexual experience and her whole body, as contrasted with the male's apparently greater tendency to focus on genital sensations and orgasm. The pervasiveness of sexual feelings in the female is associated variously—with the spread of erotic sensations from the genital region to the whole body, with special aspects of self-love, or with the woman's wish to preserve the unconscious image of the mother as body caretaker. These feelings contrast with those of the boy, who must establish distance from such internalized images of the mother in order to achieve a separate, masculine identity. If these feelings really are determined by gender, they clearly must influence the emotional attitudes that men and women bring not only to the sexual act but to the whole relationship.

Another set of "female" traits is deduced from various stages in the process of reproduction—that is, the physical sexual act, the fact of conception, the process of gestation, and breast-feeding of the infant. The theory is that, *for the female*, the sexual act indicates the qualities of being accepting, receptive, and perhaps submissive; conception indicates a tendency to incorporate; gestation indicates a nurturing quality; and breast-feeding, nurturing, closeness, and giving. *For the male*, the sexual act may be thought to indicate activity, pursuit, aggressiveness, conquest, directness, and thrust; and from the remaining stages, the ability to protect and provide for a mate (a female) and children.

From the same general source, but more abstractly derived, a characteristic frequently attributed to the female is a greater devotion to the principles and practice of monogamy and fidelity. While this idea may be more a wish than an actuality, many people have assumed that the woman, because of her responsibilities as mother and nurturer of the helpless infant, tends to be the guardian of the family unit and the arbiter of sexual "morality." For her to ignore these responsibilities is to risk disruption of the family. This view arises in part from observations of primates, among whom the mother clearly assumes these roles. Again, these concepts are frequently employed to determine the "appropriate" or "natural" role of women.

Historically in American society adulterous behavior has been condemned more sharply in the woman than in the man; similarly, desertion or neglect of the family has been regarded as more offensive in the female than in the male. These attitudes probably relate to the view of the mother as nurturer and perhaps also to the concept of the wife as property. Recently the opinion has been expressed that the standard of fidelity in women was devised by men to constrain women and preserve male dominance while permitting men to enjoy their own infidelities if they were so inclined. On the other hand, until the development of reliable methods of contraception it was the woman who incurred the potentially serious consequences of pregnancy if she engaged in sexual intercourse outside of marriage. In the last few years new attitudes have emerged which reflect a growing disenchantment with the double standard. Ironically, our society, while conventionally intolerant of infidelity, promotes and propagandizes its forerunners: flirtation, body exposure, alcohol, and other devices to decrease sexual inhibition. The female body and the female mystique are emphasized for the explicit purpose of whetting the male sexual appetite, and the very concept of seductiveness is usually associated with woman. The man is portrayed as eternally eager to engage in the sex act, and his alleged proclivity is symbolized by animal synonyms (stud, wolf, stag). There is more than a little evidence to suggest that such beliefs are assimilated by men and women in the process of growing up and that their behavior is affected by the attempts of each gender to live up to an assumed ideal.

Sexual behavior, then, is not a clear-cut phenomenon. It is a mix of physiology and anatomy, of emotions, attitudes, and expectations in one individual, reacting with a similar mix in another individual. This interaction is modified by various pressures from the broader surrounding milieu, which is itself influenced by precedents from the past, changes in the present, and interest in the future. At best, all these elements blend into an experience that is satisfying, without being harmful, to men and women singly or as a group. Opinion seems to be flowing in the direction of greater permissiveness toward sexual expression, at least on the middle- and upper-middle-class levels of our society.

Female sexual response and behavior are becoming better understood and are probably, on the whole, less different from male sexual response and behavior than scientists have thought. While there are differences, the differences within each gender group appear far more significant than those between the sexes. Among women, feelings, behavior, and goals differ enormously

and overlap those within the wide spectrum considered characteristic for men. It cannot be overstressed that the wide range of
feelings, behavior, and goals in both sexes makes rigid definitions
inappropriate and restrictive. Yet, as already noted, women—and
men—are frequently uneasy about a particular action or feeling
because of an idea that it does not meet some prevailing criterion
of acceptability for their sex.

Whether the concepts *masculinity* and *femininity* are of any
practical use is questionable, but a study of human societies
suggests that such concepts are universal. Therefore, the important question is: What consequences flow from these concepts as
they exist in our society?

The potential results of sexual behavior that only women
experience are pregnancy and childbirth. Maternity is therefore
frequently seen as quintessential "womanliness" and consequently necessary to a sense of fulfillment "as a woman." This
creates a most complicated, controversial, and as yet unsettled
issue. It has yet to be determined whether the experiences that
mean fulfillment for the majority of women are necessarily
related to biological capacity—specifically to the ability to
produce a child. There are two general views about this question.
The first is that the capacity to bear a child is so central to a
woman's being that her physiological potential is felt as a
psychological drive. Admittedly, some women do not want to
have children, but they are considered "unusual," and although
individuals among them may achieve personal fulfillment, there is
always the implication that they have simply adapted to potentially neurotic tendencies. The second view is that a woman's
fulfillment should be achieved "as a person," which bypasses any

suggestion that factors central to this fulfillment are necessarily based on her anatomy. Obviously, the two views are not an either-or proposition, but at times they are so stated. Somewhere between them lies the inescapable fact that the physiological capacity to have children, whether or not felt as a psychological drive, is something every woman must come to terms with—as a risk, a choice, or a fulfillment.

Inevitably this controversy becomes embroiled in a teleological concern. Adherents of the first view point out that if the view of woman's fulfillment "as a person" really gained sway and no woman chose to bear children, the species would become extinct and there would be no more women to be fulfilled. Proponents of the second view reply that, while this argument is logical, it is highly unlikely that all women will choose not to bear children and therefore equally unlikely that the species will die out. Because it is only recently that women, if they undertook a certain amount of sexual activity, really had the ability to prevent conception, the problem is a new one. Presumably the question is a matter of individual choice, and the answer should not be influenced by social policy; however, with the realization of the consequences of overpopulation and the emergence of the Zero Population Growth movement, there seems to have been a shift in the attitude that maternity is a necessary condition for female fulfillment. There is at least a suspicion that some of the views about the woman's "innate" desire to have children are based on unconscious feelings and currently illogical attitudes about propagating the race. Should this suspicion be confirmed, it will be necessary to review many of the concepts of female psychology. At this juncture, the question is still open.

five

COLLEGE AND AFTER

In late adolescence or early adulthood, roughly the college period, one of the most important and perhaps difficult tasks of the growing individual is the simultaneous development of autonomy and of a satisfactory sexual orientation. Becoming an independent, self-governing individual and at the same time establishing one's ability to carry on a satisfactory sexual relationship with another person is a major endeavor requiring resources that are not hampered by disabling conflicts. It is often difficult to resolve the simultaneous questions of dependence and independence. Most young people go through a process of emancipation from their families on one hand, while on the other they experiment with establishing a variety of emotional and/or sexual relationships.

The primary purpose of college is academic, but it is generally recognized that college also provides the setting for important advances in personality development.[1] For most college men and women, this means coming to some reasonably settled view of oneself as an individual and also developing some capacity for intimacy.

DEVELOPMENT OF GENDER ROLE

Except for a few colleges, where education of "the total person" is a stated goal, most academic institutions do not offer their students much that directly contributes to the development of a gender role. If a college does indirectly provide some help in the development of identity, it is likely to encourage traits traditionally associated with "maleness." For example, the pursuit of a career with single-minded determination in a highly competitive atmosphere where most of the teaching is done by a male faculty is more compatible with conventionally "masculine" than with "feminine" characteristics. To compete successfully in such a milieu, the woman often must be aggressive and must actively combat bias on the part of male teachers—a bias sometimes expressed by covert or overt refusal to take the woman student seriously.

At the same time, the male student has usually been given the opportunity and sanction for direct sexual experience, so that he is able to develop his sexual orientation. At least until recently, the woman has not been given a similar opportunity and sanction. Thus the man has occasion during his four years in college to undergo experiences which assist both his autonomous development and the establishment of his sexual orientation. Although he may as a result show evidence of great turmoil, he is the more

83

likely upon graduation to have consolidated and synthesized his personality to a considerable extent.

The woman student experiences college differently. Although she may engage in sexual experimentation, the psychological development required for her possible reproductive role (pregnancy, childbearing, and early child-rearing) is usually not confronted either directly or indirectly, and frequently is not even considered intellectually to any significant degree. The college environment is actually antipathetic to preparation for this role because if the woman is a serious student, she will usually not have the time or the opportunity to develop it. Career or job choice and various options in life style may be important for her establishment of autonomy, but they will not help her to resolve conscious or unconscious conflicts about her sexual and reproductive role. In fact, the pressure for outstanding intellectual performance may serve as a defense against undertaking the arduous task of developing a capacity for sexual intimacy. This is not to suggest that wholehearted involvement in intellectual activities is neurotic or precludes development in the sexual sphere, but it should be recognized that pursuit of a career can offer an escape from sexual anxiety and conflicts.

Conversely, undue reliance on sexual activity as a form of gratification can interfere with the development of other capacities that may be needed later in life. The extremes of such one-sided development are caricatured in the brilliant, competent, and successful woman who is largely sealed off from her instinctual life and is emotionally cold and often angry with men; and in the attractive, popular, seductive "man's woman," who is seemingly shallow, dependent, and "dumb."

The following case vignette is an example from the psycho-analysis of a woman who entered therapy in her late thirties.

Mrs. A sought help because of severe phobias which restricted her movement away from home and precluded her professional travel. Issues were raised in the analysis that traced some of her difficulties to a failure to resolve problems of autonomy and gender role. She was a capable student, elected to Phi Beta Kappa when she graduated from college. When she showed her father her Phi Beta Kappa key he said, "With that and 10 cents you can get a ride on the subway." This incident was characteristic of many experiences in which she felt her father demeaned her intellectual achievements. For Mrs. A, the "mind" was a masculine prerogative, as were particularly skills relating to mathematics or mechanical things. On the other hand, historical or more abstract pursuits, which she herself viewed as ineffectual, were permissively feminine, and she had taken a Ph.D. degree in such a field.

In her analysis, Mrs. A appreciated more fully that her father was threatened by her intellectual capacities, and she behaved as if her vitality belonged to a male part of herself. She felt that she would be unfeminine or potentially castrating to men if she were openly to show her intellectual potential. She had been able to work only at scholarly tasks which she regarded as highly obscure or "dead." She was restricted in applying her competence to more active or action-oriented fields. In addition, her mother had overestimated her capabilities and she felt that she was expected to perform in order to make up for her mother's emptiness, to supply the mother with her missing male part which at the same time threatened her father.

This struggle was being waged internally and was one source of Mrs. A's marked inhibitions and phobias. She had great difficulty asking her husband directly to accommodate her own career when it might inconvenience him. Internally, she also experienced herself as "bad" when she acted outside of her internalized model for femininity, in which there was no channel for developing an autonomous self.

In their college years most students experience some degree of emotional attachment to another person. Sexual experimentation is likely to occur and may or may not involve intercourse. For some, the experiences will be fleeting—single dates or a series of brief encounters; for others, relationships may be serious and may last for an indefinite period. Attachments may be of a homosexual or heterosexual nature. Most individuals will opt for a heterosexual orientation, but some may choose a homosexual one. The ensuing discussion primarily focuses on heterosexual relationships because, besides being statistically most likely, they inevitably highlight issues relating to gender differences. In either case the opportunity exists to learn how one's self-concept, gender identity, and sexual responsiveness work in actual practice. In the process of achieving adult sexual orientation, one's sexual relationships, both heterosexual and homosexual, may become exceedingly complex, and they will inevitably be affected by earlier events, identifications, and conflicts. It is not uncommon to find a person repeating experiences directly connected with unconscious images of masculinity and femininity formed during earlier periods, while consciously trying to develop new definitions of self. For example, people who reject the nuclear family in favor of communal living may nevertheless duplicate in their new life situation the same patterns of behavior they have rejected in their parents.

Life styles reflect many different concepts of masculinity and femininity, and certain ones will be more congenial for some people than for others, depending on how well any particular pattern, whether or not it is socially conventional, represents the best possible resolution of the diverse and sometimes conflicting interests of the person. From a psychoanalytic viewpoint, a style is appropriate (adaptive) to the extent that the behavior elected takes into account the internal as well as the external realities of the person. *Adaptive* does not mean simply conforming to a social norm or even necessarily behaving "logically," although these may be among the qualities of a particular life style. Adaptation might involve a capacity to change the environment or to search out a new and more favorable environment. No single life style can be presumed *a priori* to be "healthier" or "more adaptive" for everyone. What is adaptive not only may differ from one person to another, but also may change for any given person as development proceeds throughout the life cycle. This case vignette illustrates some of these points:

Jane was a senior student working toward completion of her honors thesis. She had a strong interest in math and physical science and generally did well. She had been supported by her professors and her thesis adviser in this work, although she had had a number of near-arguments with her adviser, in which she felt he was not taking her seriously enough and had not given her sufficient credit for her independence of thought. Jane was concerned that as a woman she was not expected to make use of her math and physics skills in the future. It was very important to her to "amount to something" and to attain prominence in her field, yet she was very sensitive to any implications that might challenge her "femininity."

87

Jane's boy friend was also a science student, in graduate school. Recently they had talked of getting married. She felt in considerable conflict—felt that she might be unfair to him if they did get married, despite her strong conviction that a two-career family was possible. Actually he was very supportive of her working after marriage, as several women in his family had professional careers.

Jane came for counseling help after she blew up when a professor questioned her on a point of data. She felt she had overreacted and that her sensitivity threatened the possibility of obtaining a fellowship. She described the ways in which "the system" worked to the disadvantage of women students, the overt and covert discrimination. She also recognized how quick she was to feel threatened or attacked, and her great sensitivity to depreciation and slights. The psychiatrist asked her whether she might not share the ambivalence toward achievement she so readily saw in others.

Jane was an attractive, lively girl. She had always been the good student in her family, the youngest of four children. Her mother, a middle-class housewife, had played down Jane's intellectual achievements, although proud of her good record at school. She used to tell Jane not to be a "bookworm," not to read so much—the boys wouldn't like it. Jane's father was an unsuccessful but intelligent businessman. For years he was submerged in work. When he was home or at family gatherings, he would speak mostly to other men, including Jane's boy friend. Her mother deferred to her father, insisting that she couldn't follow the abstract conversations, and retreated to the kitchen. Jane vowed she would not be like her mother. She would succeed beyond her father's attainments. She worried that marriage might be a trap, but at the same time felt genuinely drawn to her boy friend.

After several counseling interviews, Jane saw the degree to which she herself had internalized her family attitude that intellectual achievement would be aggressive, improper, and unfeminine. She herself had doubts about her competence. However, her awareness of the intensity of her self-doubt made her less vulnerable to implied criticism from others. A fellow student commented that she seemed less abrasive and provocative of late.

Getting to know the family of a woman professor helped Jane envision the possibility of a kind of marriage different from that of her parents. When she went to visit her family for a holiday, she felt acutely conscious of her mother's sense of entrapment. But this led her to feel some sympathy for her mother and less of the alienation she had felt before. The deeper sources of her self-doubt were not explored, but were acknowledged. Nevertheless, she functioned more comfortably and completed her work.

Each individual must integrate the two processes—the forming of emotional relationships with others and the establishing of himself or herself as an autonomous person. These two are by no means unrelated. It is not uncommon for the woman (or man) to transfer dependent feelings directly from parents to partner, which often places strains on the relationship that it cannot endure. For various reasons, relationships may develop rapidly and end just as rapidly. Sometimes the relationship may be opportunistic or convenient and fade when circumstances change. Through experience, however, each person learns something about his or her emotional and sexual response, which can make succeeding relationships more satisfactory. Nevertheless, for some people, unconscious factors will prevent the improvement of relationships simply by successive experiences.

In the past young adults usually went through a series of courting rituals such as dates and dances, and exposure to each other before they were engaged was rather artificial. Today it is not unusual for a couple to decide to live together for a time without any permanent commitment. In some ways this arrangement gives them a preview of marriage and a chance to test out their reactions to each other in a very intense way. Probably it is most likely to succeed if each partner has already achieved a certain autonomy, a capacity for intimacy, and a satisfactory sexual response. Otherwise, as has been pointed out, this new arrangement may simply be a continuation of an effort to remain dependent, with the lover substituted for the parents.

CAREER AND MARRIAGE

Not unnaturally, as a male-female relationship develops, the question of its permanence may arise. Traditionally, for many the end of college has been a logical time to consider marriage. Nowadays, of course, a permanent relationship does not necessarily imply marriage. The term *marriage* is used here because many of its implications are so clear-cut. But much of the discussion that follows would apply equally to a nonlegalized relationship that the partners considered permanent. Formerly most women felt themselves faced with a choice between a serious career commitment involving professional or graduate school, and a marriage involving full-time motherhood, at least for some years. The few women who chose to combine marriage with a career had to struggle with difficult decisions during the years when many of their friends were having babies. They faced the dilemma of whether to interrupt their work for a few years to have children or to continue work during this period and make do with various complicated arrangements for household help and child care. Until recently, this last choice has been an unusual one for women.

The need to choose between one or the other of these life patterns seems unfortunate. It tends to polarize the marital sphere so that the home is for women and the outside world is for men. It is based on the assumption that there is no way of combining a serious career with the pleasures and responsibilities of bringing up children. For the past few years more women students than formerly have been choosing to follow a relatively uninterrupted career while attempting to work out some pattern of marital living that will make this possible.

The question of marriage is important because it is still the preferred choice for most women. Although there is currently some evidence of a trend toward remaining single, the overwhelming majority of women today are married or would like to be. Marriage provides companionship, which is important to most people; it provides a stable environment for raising children, which most women want to have; and it meets the needs of women for protection and security. It also meets the needs of men for domestic support. Despite the literary convention that men are reluctant bridegrooms, the man in many instances presses the woman to enter marriage.

Most college women today want both marriage and career. It is often pointed out that they lack models in the preceding generation, partly because many career women of the last generation did not marry. College women tend to assume either that these older women had no opportunities to marry, in which case the students do not want to identify with them; or that the older women, if single by choice, chose not to have children, which students today are not usually willing to do, at least at the outset.

Although a stable and fulfilling marriage with mutual support may offer a highly adaptive situation, particularly in relation to the children, the role of mother-housewife may also be used as a defense. In the process of being a "feminine" woman and a "good mother," a woman may effectively isolate herself from the competitive world, and in so doing she may be responding to her underlying fears—for example, anxiety about competing. It may not be necessary or desirable to face such fears head on, but still, this is a choice, influenced by unconscious as well as conscious factors. This choice may not become a problem until later in life, when the children are grown and the homemaker role becomes less adaptive. At that time the woman's anxieties may make it difficult to select another life style even if she consciously desires to make a change.

Competitive rivalry with siblings, with a parent, or with some other family member provides the earliest basis for feelings which are later revived and reinforced by a variety of social situations. In some degree such feelings are universal, but they are expressed in very different ways by different individuals. The girl who has handled her feelings of competition with her brother by submissiveness, or who has repressed her feelings of rivalry with her mother in the process of resolving her Oedipal feelings toward her father, may develop strong inhibitions about expressing aggression later in her life. She may feel disturbed when confronted with a type of work that demands personal competition from her. Some studies done at Harvard and the University of Michigan indicate that women fear success.[2] Although later studies have partially questioned this,[3] fear of success seems to be a factor in a rather complex reaction.[4] A similar study of men revealed that men also have anxieties but of a quite different nature.[5]

In contrast to most men, college women associate academic success with unpleasant consequences. Men may have to cope with similar anxieties about competition and the expression of aggression, but they are also supported by the knowledge that the aggressive, competitive man is a social ideal. A woman who chooses the socially acceptable role of full-time wife and mother, and thus avoids confronting unresolved conflicts, has also found an acceptable position in which she can maintain a certain degree of dependency, which may be important to her psychological balance.

Similarly, there are both positive and defensive aspects to choosing a career. A career provides possibilities for the development of intellectual, social, and other skills, but a woman may not choose it solely because of a desire for fulfillment and the development of her potential. A career permits a woman to avoid the areas of traditional femininity, which may be fraught with conflict for her, because of earlier life experiences. She may be apprehensive about her sexual functioning and about her capacity "to be a woman," which she equates with bearing and raising children and perhaps avoiding the mistakes she feels her own mother has made.

This is not to say that the motivation for either choice is "neurotic," but rather that choice is rarely a simple matter—and it is determined by many factors, some adaptive and some defensive. If one wishes to make a choice in one's life involving change, it becomes important to be aware of the functions that previously followed patterns have served.

In any relationship between people, each person's needs are important. For men as well as women, a socially acceptable life pattern may serve defensive purposes. Rigidly held "masculinity" may be a defense against unconscious passive and dependent feelings which would be very threatening if they reached consciousness. A hard-driving businessman who is admired and considered a model of success may also be using his activity to defend against feelings of passivity. In a marriage where the partners are complementary from the start, any later change in one partner may create real problems if it disrupts patterns that have gratified the other. Thus, if the wife has initially chosen to be a housewife and later decides to pursue a career, the marital readjustment may involve far more than simply finding supervision for the children or a housekeeper to prepare supper. This case vignette illustrates how the husband may be involved:

Charles and Dorothy came from relatively wealthy upper-middle-class families. They were married shortly after graduation from college. Charles went to work for a bank at a good salary. Dorothy had not followed any career direction very seriously in college and was content to establish their home and devote herself to volunteer activities of the Junior League.

Their relationship was a good one. They enjoyed several sports together and had a pleasant circle of friends. They assumed they would have a child right away, but Dorothy did not conceive immediately. After the first year, she found herself rather restless and not really satisfied by her volunteer activities. Rather unexpectedly she was offered a full-time job as an administrative assistant at a social agency where she had volunteered, and somewhat on impulse she accepted it.

At first Charles had no objections and seemed pleased at the prospect of increased family income. Gradually, however, tensions began to develop in the marriage, marked by a series of rather heated arguments. Sometimes these spats seemed to be about minor matters of housekeeping, such as the beds not being made or supper not being ready, and sometimes about financial matters, such as the need for a new refrigerator, which Dorothy wanted and Charles felt was unnecessary. When Dorothy replaced the old one, using her own earnings, a really serious fight was precipitated, which left Charles quite depressed.

Discussion of their tensions with a marriage counselor revealed that Charles had a rather rigid concept of marital roles. When his role as the provider was threatened by Dorothy's earnings and subsequent greater independence, his feelings of masculinity were undermined and he found himself involuntarily taking positions that were essentially irrational. Concomitantly, he found himself inexplicably depressed and angry when Dorothy's role as housekeeper, cook, and sympathetic listener (essentially his mother's role), which fulfilled his unconscious dependency needs, was altered. The original marital relationship had been a highly satisfactory one for Charles. When Dorothy changed her role, he found it difficult to adapt to the new conditions.

Changes in a marital relationship as time passes are almost inevitable, but some are more difficult to adapt to than others.

Those that modify fundamental patterns which one partner had found gratifying are more likely to cause strain.

PREGNANCY AND THE FIRST CHILD

Adaptability in marriage is inevitably further complicated when a child is added. As long as there are no children, a young couple can function with relatively loose definitions of their roles as husband and wife. Even when both are students or both are working, it is not particularly difficult to function in a parallel way, to share household chores, and to enjoy similar goals of personal fulfillment or commitment to work.

In this period of marriage there need be no contradictions between how the partners work out their life and conventional expectations. But the first pregnancy and the birth of the first child bring an unavoidable change. The traditional American expectation has been that the woman will stay at home and care for the child while the man works to provide financial support. If the tradition is followed, the woman experiences a sharper change from previous marital patterns than does the man. But when the woman wants to continue to work outside the home, she precipitates a break with conventional expectations that in itself may create problems.

The experience of pregnancy for a woman is one of potential upheaval as well as of gratification. With the first pregnancy she changes from being a daughter to being a mother. Her relationship with her own mother is revived—sometimes by a conscious longing for her mother, sometimes by the emergence of conflicts which make it difficult for her to see herself as a mother. The pregnancy affects her self-image and stirs up problems about her femininity which may have temporarily receded during the previous equilibrium.

The responsibility of care for another human being brings a new seriousness to choices about how to live. Once a baby is on its way, there is no turning back from this responsibility. How it is handled depends on the future parents, but a couple can no longer make choices about life style as casually or abstractly as before. Unconscious feelings about their own early lives with their parents are revived, and these may well conflict with their conscious theoretical ideas about how to live. The impact may be more abrupt and far-reaching for the wife, but the husband too may find that his expectations have shifted. Contradictions may arise between his conscious intention of creating a kind of family relationship different from the one he knew and unconscious influences causing him to repeat earlier family patterns. The following example illustrates such an unanticipated development:

During John's early years his father had been almost totally occupied with his business, which was on the verge of failing. He was almost never at home, and when at home he was irritable and fatigued. John determined that his child's experience would be different. Consequently, when the baby was born, John deliberately shared the activities of feeding and bathing the baby. He found, however, that his patience was frequently tried and he experienced emotions of anger toward the baby that were frightening. Without really being aware of the process, he began devising a series of chores and errands he "had" to do the moment the baby needed attention.

When his withdrawal from involvement with the baby was brought to his attention, he realized that he had been repeating his father's pattern without really knowing why.

The husband's relationship to his wife has to include their common child, who, though wanted, may still seem an intruder to them both. Theoretical ideas about how one wants to live and bring up children are put to the test, at first in anticipation, then by the real demands and needs of a real child and by the parents' feelings toward the child.

Pregnancy presents special problems to the active, competent woman whose self-image is that of someone able to cope with, to master, and to stay in control of life situations. Pregnancy, while not an illness, usually involves seeing a physician, and this may be her first experience as a "patient." She is vulnerable to the symptoms, mood changes, and other unexpected physical and psychological experiences of the pregnant state. It may be disconcerting to her, as well as surprisingly gratifying, to identify with other women in such a widely shared experience. From these new experiences she may eventually develop the potential for greater empathy with others. She may feel a sense of identification with and greater understanding of her mother. Even women who have had an abortion for an unwanted pregnancy sometimes remark that just the experience of being pregnant, even briefly, has made them more aware of their female identity and left them with greater tolerance and empathy for other women.

There may be a variety of reasons for the mother's decision to work or to continue to work after the baby is born. One is, of course, economic necessity. A woman may also feel she wants to work for a number of reasons—to earn money, to fill time, or to avoid the tensions and anxieties of staying home and satisfying the demands of small children. These motivations differ markedly from those of working because of dedication to a career or the wish to develop potential. Even a woman who has a career may be expressing a mixture of motives, and being "required" to work may be a welcome solution for someone who is uncertain or beset by conflicts. It may be particularly welcome to a woman who feels under pressure, either unconscious or conscious, to stay home and care for the child on a full-time basis. For the woman who has no choice about working, the decision may be easier, but the inner conflict is no less unsettling. In fact, rigid expectations in either direction create problems for the woman.

A wife who is seriously committed to working introduces many complexities into the arrangements of family life for herself and for her husband. Our society is not really prepared for this contingency. Priorities have to be set and reset, and decisions made and made again, as to the relative importance of particular activities with children and concentration on work. Inventiveness and resourcefulness are important in resolving these complexities, but so are time, money, and support from others—to say nothing of family models showing how such arrangements have been worked out by others without detriment to children or the marital relationship. In some instances the couple may have to apply pressure to change institutional regulations or policies. It is certainly very important that both wife and husband be flexible in their expectations of how the home and family operate.

Many different solutions can be—and have been—found.

Employing domestic help is one. For child care, help may be available in the form of a transient baby-sitter or a live-in sitter who exchanges certain services for room and board, or, occasionally but not often, a full-time housekeeper. For housecleaning, a houseworker or cleaning service may be retained on a regular basis. In some localities there are "accommodaters" who will prepare a meal, serve it, and clean up afterward. One of these services on a regular basis provides time for the parents to engage in other activities. Outside the home, day-care centers have become increasingly popular and available, although generally they remain rather scarce.

To some extent, the children themselves may be used as helpers more than they customarily are in middle-class families of small size. In earlier times it was not uncommon for a child of six or seven to be entrusted with the major care and supervision of a younger sibling in a large family.

One currently popular solution is a shift in the nature of tasks shared by the husband. With the exception of breast-feeding, there is virtually no household duty that cannot be performed by a man. A reorganization of household chores based on his participation may free essential hours for the woman who must meet the demands of an outside work schedule. This plan, however, presupposes that the husband is able and willing to share the tasks. More is involved than the logistics of who does the cooking or the dishes or who cares for the baby at any given time. There have to be important changes in how the man and woman regard each other and relate to each other. He must give up some of his expectations that *his* supper will be prepared on time, *his* laundry done promptly, and so on.

The man may also feel threatened by the implication that if he allows himself to take part in domestic activities, he will no longer be "masculine." If his sense of masculinity is shaky or is dependent on the approval of other men, he may become upset if he is teased about his domestic role. Furthermore, caretaking activities demand patience and the open expression of positive feelings, combined with the ability to respond to the child's needs, which at any given moment may be urgent, without feeling severely deprived of one's own fulfillment. Traditionally these abilities are all associated with feminine qualities. Yet if men are to function effectively in these roles, they will have to develop the capacity to find satisfaction in using similar abilities. Moreover, household tasks can be shared effectively only when the husband makes a serious and sustained effort. The woman's problems cannot be resolved if the husband "plays" at child care when he feels like it or does the dishes as a "favor" when he has no work of his own to do or when there is nothing interesting to watch on television.

However, the crucial question that continues to concern the woman who goes to work while raising children is: What is the psychological effect of the arrangement on the child? Most parents are deeply concerned with the development of the child, and most of them are aware of the psychological theory that the first years of the child's life are especially important in providing the basis for later healthy emotional development. As has been mentioned, this theory has been interpreted by some to mean that a mother should devote her full time to child care in the first few years.

Recent attempts to refute this interpretation have stressed the *quality* of mothering rather than full-time motherhood, but without defining what the quality of mothering should be. The fact is that no one really knows the key components of effective mothering or of providing a "proper" maternal environment for the child. There is evidence to suggest that full-time attendance by the mother is not necessary, but no one has clear guidelines on what is necessary, although we know from clinical experience that a consistent relationship between the child and a primary adult is extremely important for the child's development.

Despite the lack of clear, scientific information about the effects on her child of a mother's working, our society in general considers child care to be the responsibility of the mother. The woman who adopts a nontraditional pattern of family living is made to feel guilty by all kinds of people—neighbors, friends, husband, mother, mother-in-law, and children—who reproach her for leaving home. Her guilt feelings may reinforce unconscious feelings left over from her own childhood development. A woman who genuinely feels it is important for a child to be able to separate from her when she does household errands thoughtfully and carefully helps the child to do so, secure in her conviction that she is being a good mother. The same mother, however, may have many conflicts when the errands are replaced by a job and she must leave the child at regular times. Women who have had problems with separation in their own lives feel particularly vulnerable; they identify with the child, sometimes inappropriately, and may not in the long run be helpful to the child's development.

Another important unknown factor directly concerns the sharing of child care and its relation to the child's unconscious psychological identification. An attempt has already been made here to describe the complex manner in which a girl or a boy develops identification with female or male figures in the environment. There are indications that these psychosexual identifications are fundamental to a sound sense of self and to adult functioning as a male or as a female, at least sexually. If mother and father divide all tasks equally, will the child have a clear-cut sense of two sexes simply from their anatomical differences? And if not, does it matter?

Cross-cultural studies suggest that every society makes relatively clear gender distinctions, but we do not really know what the effect on children would be if these distinctions were, to all intents and purposes, functionally blurred. It is tempting to suggest that a parent should first of all show what it is to be a human being and secondarily, but not inconsequentially, show what it is to be male or female without being bound to a stereotyped view of these roles. Unfortunately, the meaning of this suggestion is not clear unless one presupposes that there are certain traits characteristic of each sex, a belief which suggests the existence of stereotypes.

Despite the burgeoning population-control movement, social pressure for parenthood remains very strong. A woman who genuinely wants to stay home with her children during their early years may find it difficult to re-enter a professional field some time later, so she is faced with a difficult choice. If she is seriously interested in a career, the conflict may be external as well as internal. The problems of providing care for the children and the household are compounded by the requirements of many careers. Consider the following statement by a woman Ph.D.

Child care was always an issue when the children were younger. I relied a lot on baby-sitters, and my kids still take me to task for one really bad nursery school they were in. I owe my dissertation to one woman friend who did a lot of substitute mothering (they could then get by without sitters) while I put in an eighteen-hour day for a couple of months. I've always been fortunate in working with people who were most flexible about time off for getting kids to the doctor's, school conferences, and so on.

Time for research in a medical school is difficult to come by *for anyone*. The primary demands are for clinical work and teaching; but promotion and tenure depend upon publication. The men who publish do so by putting in many hours after work. Recently I have been unwilling to put in that kind of "killer" schedule—at least until my children are gone, which won't be very many more years. By then, however, I may well have jeopardized my chances of promotion and tenure, which means termination.

In a given field, flexible work arrangements may be impossible, and part-time work may mean lower status and be less interesting and rewarding than a full schedule. Moreover, the woman may be vulnerable to the accusation that she is not "a good mother." A working mother is always ready to feel guilty about this whenever anything goes wrong. Because she may feel more strongly than the full-time mother that she has to do everything perfectly, her tensions and burdens may be greater still. The following quotation is from a paper written by a woman about the problems of a woman physician:

To perform in a traditional medical career and carry out the activities of a traditional wife and mother is clearly impossible, and one has to develop alternative solutions and roles. In the past, the availability of household help to the middle-class or professional woman allowed for the possibility of greater independence. Current social patterns demand different life styles and a reconsideration of these traditional family roles so that a woman who becomes a physician does not have to be a "special" person who must essentially perform two or more full-time jobs.

Women in medicine who also have families face the same problems as women with other serious work commitments and families. In addition to the demands of the profession, there are the complexities of functioning in a deviant way from the pattern in a particular community. It is easy to feel guilty if something doesn't go right at home—guilt which is reinforced by comments of sometimes hostile neighbors (who may be deeply envious). Even in a friendly environment some sense of conflict is potentially very close to the surface. "Am I doing the right thing?" is a latent question. Constant reassessments take place, weighing the value of a professional meeting, for instance, against the disruption of family patterns. Most of these issues are solvable; it is enormously helpful if there are others doing the same thing and pursuing similar solutions. Other women in medicine serving as role models offering peer support are immensely important.[6]

This is true in fields other than medicine. Furthermore, there is the "pull" of the mothering role; it provides satisfactions that may interfere with career demands, as this statement from a faculty woman indicates:

Now that I've had a child I realize I wouldn't want to be away full-time from my family, which, Women's Lib notwithstanding, has become a very important part of my life. This makes publications, so necessary for academic progress, much harder to produce, especially in science, which requires large blocks of time away from home. I'm not sure how I'll resolve this eventually.

Women need to be allowed not only to find life styles that may differ from those of people who are important to them, but to observe a diversity of other people who can serve as role models and teachers. These can be of immense help in deciding to adopt a certain life style and also in providing solutions for various practical problems because they themselves are real-life illustrations of how such problems have been solved successfully. It is also important for men to know older women who have worked out solutions in nontraditional ways. A prominent woman sociologist has suggested that someone should write a kind of how-to-do-it handbook that would offer suggestions for coping with problems peculiar to the working mother. There are data indicating that a very important factor in a woman's choice to work outside the home and to continue working after she is a mother may be that her own mother worked and that her relationship with her mother was satisfactory.[7]

Where this is true, the woman has an excellent and highly influential model, as is illustrated by a further quotation from the woman Ph.D. quoted earlier:

Important last thought—many women in my field have had enormous conflicts over the professional vs. female issue, and I think it's been responsible for many giving up before reaching the degree. I had my share of that, but it was easier for several reasons: (1) I had made it as a wife and mother. (2) My own mother is an engineer and her example was very useful to me. (3) Despite my worst fears I continue to be confirmed as a woman (in the best sense of that word) by male friends and colleagues.

Obviously, many women do not have mothers who can be role models in this respect, but some of them can find other older women to serve as substitutes.

LATER PHASES OF CHILD-REARING

Babies make special demands on their families; toddlers and older children make different ones. At each stage of the child's development parental adaptations must be different, and they are constantly changing.[8] From the very beginning until many years later all children need care while the mother or principal caretaking person is absent. It becomes increasingly difficult in modern life to find a housekeeper or nursemaid for this purpose. Day-care facilities provide only a partial answer, and they are not widely available.

In some families it is possible for the father to share equally in the care of the child and household duties. This arrangement may be only expedient, or it may be a valuable method of shifting away from traditional masculine and feminine roles and may contribute to more meaningful family relationships. At present, however, few fathers are able or willing to share equally in family tasks if they must work part-time to do so.

In some working-class families the father has traditionally

shared the tasks, only not for ideological reasons but because the two parents work alternate shifts. But it is difficult to have a meaningful family life under such conditions, and the parents may rarely see each other. Fathers who do share child care are sometimes surprised and even a little guilty about how much they enjoy it. And this sharing can lead to unexpected problems, such as the development of subtle competition between mother and father for the position of "best mother." The woman who initially saw the process of sharing primarily as a means of lightening her burdens may suddenly find herself feeling threatened.

Today many young couples are exploring alternative ways of organizing family life and child care. They are especially interested in permitting the mother and father to share more evenly in the care of children. For example, in middle-class neighborhoods with a large population of academic and professional people, fathers as well as mothers come to help on school trips to museums or other points of interest. Fathers now help out on other school projects. But it is not yet clear how widespread these changes are.

As children grow older, the hours that must be devoted to their actual care and supervision decrease because of school attendance and other activities. But nevertheless a child may become more insistent on having a parent rather than a baby-sitter available when he or she wants or needs an adult. The child wants the particular qualities the parent has to offer and is not mollified by the presence of a relatively unknown person. Consequently, demands on the parents may not diminish. One woman who seems to have worked out a reasonably satisfactory solution is still concerned by this problem:

Phyllis is a married thirty-one-year-old medical student who has two children. Her mother is a housewife whom she describes as strong, stubborn, and a perfectionist, with whom she has a subservient relationship. Her father, who was brought up in an Eastern culture, has been entirely wrapped up in his business life without outside interests. She has very little in common with him on a day-to-day basis but she is proud of his praise and avoids his displeasure at almost any cost. Both parents have a high-school education.

Because of her enjoyment of science in college Phyllis first thought of medicine as a career, and her parents' attitudes played an important part in the final choice. She states, "My father seemed to respect physicians so highly. . . . I suppose I thought it would make me feel less subservient to my mother." Both parents encouraged this career choice. Her final decision was not made, however, until she married her physician husband. She felt that an important factor in the decision was having a husband who was willing to make the sacrifices necessary for her to continue her career. Furthermore, she had studied in other areas of medical science and found she was unhappy in a laboratory setting.

Medical school has not changed Phyllis's concept of herself as a woman; she still sees herself as a wife and mother first. She is concerned about the amount of time she spends away from her children. "We have a good nurse, and all I can do is hope that it will not be too detrimental. If it is, I will stop my career. But I feel quite certain that, rather than my children suffering from my absence, it will be I who suffer because I will not see them as much as I would like." Going back to work part-time shortly after delivery is not detrimental to the children, she feels. "I believe firmly that there are no bad consequences so long as the child knows the mother loves him and during the time she is home she gives him the attention and care he needs." She looks forward to her internship and a residency in her area of specialization.

In short, there seems to be no easy or uniform solution to the woman's problem of combining career and family. Various life and family patterns may be found which fit the personalities concerned, resolve the problems, and are appropriate to the relationships. And for a given couple these patterns may change over time, as one phase of marriage and family development succeeds another. Flexibility on the part of both partners and their refusal to accept rigid gender roles will make life easier. An ability to tolerate social disapproval with equanimity is also important, for the partners may well be subjected to hostility or criticism by friends or relatives. It is important to establish value priorities, to compromise, and to accept lowered standards in some areas, especially when children claim attention. Parents may want more time with their children and find themselves in conflict when outside jobs or necessary household chores interfere with purely recreational activities involving the children.

A couple is more than just two people, and there cannot be total freedom of action for either member. It is essential to recognize this. If one member has total freedom, the relationship is that of master and servant instead of being reciprocal. Therefore every couple living together experiences some conflict requiring compromise, and it is a question whether each of them can be equally fulfilled. Presumably the arrangement, on balance, provides more pleasure than pain, but it inevitably involves some sharing of work that is either tedious or unpleasant. To be able to do this without feeling exploited or frustrated, the partners must be mature and must invest a considerable amount of energy in resolving the inevitable problems.

There are many pressures and temptations for a woman to give up working, or at least to declare a moratorium until the children are grown, and thus to retreat from the complexities of combining career and family. It is often more socially acceptable for a woman to drop her career than it is for a man, unless economic or psychological necessity requires her to work. A paper by one professional woman refers to the "regressive pull of motherhood," noting that regression may have started in pregnancy and is often continued after childbirth.[9] In fact, any disruption of the balance of the woman's life, such as difficulties in making arrangements for child care or housekeeping, the demands of the husband's career, or the need to move geographically may be enough to make her give up her career. And the competitive nature of many work situations may discourage her from continuing. For a woman it is possible to stay home, care for her children, and avoid the conflicts of the marketplace while leading a life that is approved by convention. This is the preferred choice for many women, and one that should not be deprecated. It may, however, reflect a desire to retreat from conflict, and this aspect of the choice needs to be emphasized, because so many factors press toward giving up outside work.

Men as well as women may be disturbed by the pressures and anxieties inherent in their careers, may experience problems with achievement and success, but in our society men live with cultural expectations which are just as limiting as those of women. They cannot avoid competitive strains without running the risk of significantly diminishing themselves in their own eyes or in the eyes of those around them. Until now, however, they have not had much responsibility in the domestic sphere; their obligations may have been difficult to meet, but they have not had to oppose traditional expectations in order to meet them.

Finally, the needs of the child must be considered in any family arrangement: the complete equation for the satisfactory distribution of family responsibilities must balance the needs, gratifications, and capacities of all three—mother, father, and child.

six

PSYCHOTHERAPY AND PSYCHOTHERAPISTS

Although formal psychotherapy is experienced by only a small percentage of college women, a book by psychiatrists about problems of the educated woman must discuss the impact of psychotherapy on women. The term *psychotherapy* currently covers a wide range of approaches and therapies. In this discussion it refers primarily to a psychoanalytically oriented, nondirective therapy, utilizing a modified technique of free association, in which an attempt is made to uncover certain unconscious feelings and to trace patterns of reaction with the aim of achieving psychological insight for the patient. Two facts must be recognized immediately: (1) that the majority of psychotherapists, on college campuses and off, are male; and (2) that psychotherapy, though often striving for neutrality or a nondirective approach, does have an implicit value system. The latter fact may be denied or disguised, and the therapist's values may frequently be difficult or impossible to define precisely; nevertheless, they exist.

As already noted, Freud's work has markedly influenced psychiatry and psychology in this country, and, intentionally or not, some of his views have helped to shape prevailing definitions of femininity as well as to imply certain "normative states" fundamental to the mental health of women and to their maturation, fulfillment, or adaptation. A recent study suggests that many clinicians today view their female patients in much the same way that Freud viewed his many years ago.[1] This study tested 79 therapists (46 male and 33 female psychiatrists, psychologists, and social workers), using a questionnaire designed to reveal sex-role stereotypes. The test listed 122 pairs of traits in opposition—for example: "very subjective . . . very objective"; "not at all aggressive . . . very aggressive."

Investigators asked the subjects to rate a healthy male, a healthy female, and a healthy adult (sex unspecified) according to each of these traits, on a scale from 1 to 7. They found that

> There was close agreement among these clinicians on the attributes they felt characterized men, women, and adults.
>
> There were no major differences between the opinions of male and female clinicians.
>
> Clinicians had standards of mental health for men that differed from those for women. Their standards for "healthy adult man" corresponded to those for "healthy adult"; but those for "healthy woman" differed from both by including submissiveness, emotionality, susceptibility to influence, sensitivity to hurts, excitability, conceit about their appearance, and dependency, coupled with a lack of adventurousness, competitiveness, aggressiveness, and objectivity.

At the very least these findings suggest that clinicians, be they male or female, are influenced by stereotypes of women and men, of which they are conscious. Although this study needs to be repeated and the specific group of therapists tested is not described, the findings cannot be ignored. And it is difficult to imagine that the stereotypes these therapists share do not influence the course of their psychotherapy.

One may ask how these stereotypes, or values based on them, are transmitted from therapist to patient in the course of psychotherapy, particularly in a therapy which is nondirective. The answer is not clear-cut, but probably the route of transmission lies through the interpretations of the therapist or the statements of the patient chosen by the therapist for exploration.[2] As has been noted, individuals make choices for a variety of reasons, which, from the psychological point of view, can be thought of as adaptive or defensive (although probably most choices represent a combination of both). Most psychotherapists would take the position that a choice made primarily for defensive reasons is less constructive, more likely to prove unsatisfactory in the long run, and perhaps even more pathological, than one made for adaptive reasons.

To oversimplify for the moment, a woman may choose marriage and motherhood, the more traditional female role, and if the therapist sees this choice as adaptive, he will not challenge it. Certainly the role gratifies very real needs for creativity, dependency, and passivity. However, if the therapist feels that the choice is being made because the woman is anxious about pursuing a career or frightened of success, initiative, competition, or independence, he may question it. The reverse choice is more likely to be questioned, the choice against marriage and motherhood. The therapist who feels that total fulfillment for a woman requires these experiences probably looks on the choice against them as a defensive one and may strongly question the patient's underlying feelings, and he may thus influence the patient to reconsider and perhaps change her mind.

Or if a woman in college elects to major in engineering, and, in exploring the reasons for her choice, the therapist focuses on the fact that her father is an engineer, questions may be raised about her "masculine" identification. But let us suppose that the father is a child psychiatrist and the woman chooses a major in child study. This choice might be accepted without question or comment by the therapist, who unconsciously feels it is an appropriate choice. Presumably, if it is reasonable to raise the issue of masculine identification in the first instance, it is equally reasonable to raise it in the second. Needless to say, these simplifications of a very complex process are not examples of approved psychotherapeutic technique but rather attempts to show how a therapist's unconscious (and sometimes conscious) values may be transmitted to a patient.

It should be noted that any college student, male or female, who is attempting a redefinition of gender role does so within his or her own developmental context. Thus, what may be "liberated" or "individuated" for a college freshman may be quite inappropriate for a college senior. Although this fact should be self-evident, it is not always considered by either students or therapists. Nevertheless, in a very real sense, explorations of identity should never be viewed as closed. It is to be hoped, even to be desired, that they are viewed as a lifelong process, particularly within the context of a close relationship with another person. Such explorations continue as two people define their roles in living together, marriage, work, the continuation of their education (who works while who goes to school), deciding whether or not to have children, how many to have, and how they should be raised (within the home or with the help of ancillary facilities such as day-care centers). A sense of openness about gender role definition should be a vital value for therapists in consultation, just as we have suggested it should be for parents in child-rearing. Settling for the old stereotyped style of raising a "real" boy or a "real" girl is certainly more comfortable, but it seems to perpetuate many of the values that lead to later difficulties with gender role.

To discuss these matters is not to suggest, as some women recently have suggested, that psychotherapy is no longer a viable source of help for women. What it does suggest is that therapists should re-examine some of their own values. More particularly, they must learn to recognize the stereotypes about gender role they hold consciously or unconsciously, must become more sensitive to unconscious influences shaping their own values, must struggle to eliminate the power strategies sometimes at play in therapy, or at least be aware how these limiting factors may be inadvertently introduced into therapy. Having gone through this evaluative process (and many experienced therapists have already done so), any therapist will be better able to help women and men redefine their gender roles, explore their options as human beings, and attain greater individuation and autonomy. In fact psychotherapy and psychoanalysis, although of limited availability, are, when freed from the burden of stereotypes, useful ways of clarifying unconscious determinants that bear on the manifest problem of gender role, and of removing some of the internal barriers that interfere with women's utilization of their full capacities.

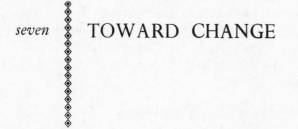

seven   TOWARD CHANGE

In Women's Roles

Some women are beginning to challenge one or more aspects of the stereotyped gender roles in themselves and perhaps secondarily in men. They may do this for internal reasons, perhaps through positive identification with an older woman who works; or for external reasons—perhaps because of an academic course on women's roles they may have taken, or because of the influence on their thinking of one of the Women's Liberation groups, or because of new demands made on them by divorce or widowhood. The outcome of their challenge will inevitably influence their relationships with other people. Some of the consequences of a woman's redefinition of her gender role in relation to herself, other women, and men call for exploration.

The woman's relationship to herself. The social position of women makes it difficult for them to achieve self-esteem. The American psychologist Gerhart Saenger writes:

> . . . the existence of a sound self-esteem, which in large measure depends upon successful identification with one's group, is fundamental for the development of well-adjusted personality. The feeling of being accepted and accepting one's group is basic for the individual's security. Where the group is considered inferior by the larger society, and membership in it related to deprivations, a positive identification with the group and the development of strong ties of belonging become difficult.[1]

Saenger believes that a minority group tends to accept the beliefs of the dominant group, and as a result the minority has conflicting feelings about the imposed inferior role and feels a lack of self-worth. *Even in individuals who do not accept these negative beliefs, the impact of prejudice and discrimination lowers self-esteem and heightens insecurity.*

Two studies have led to the conclusion that college "men and women esteem men significantly more highly than women"[2] and that

> . . . men were considered frank and straightforward in social relations, intellectually rational and competent, and bold and effective in dealing with the environment. Men's undesirable characteristics are largely limited to excesses of these traits. The stereotype of women embraces the social amenities, emotional warmth, and a concern for affairs besides the material. In addition, women are regarded as guilty of snobbery and irrational and unpleasant emotionality. Male subjects particularly emphasized men's desirable characteristics; females emphasized women's neuroticism.[3]

The American psychologist Kenneth Keniston and others have studied women who are trying to change and redefine their sex roles through greater individuation, autonomy, and independence. He points out that these women justly complain of having no models for what they are trying to do.[4] The American sociologist Alice Rossi has noted that it is acceptable for such women to admit conflicting feelings toward roles that are optional, such as that of "career woman." [5] The more important the role is considered to be for the maintenance and survival of society, the greater the likelihood that the woman will repress her feelings against it and will erect unconscious barriers to prevent its expression. Another American psychologist, Anne Steinmann, studied seventy-five college women, who indicated that they perceived themselves and their "ideal women" as essentially alike, with equal components of passive and active orientation; but they perceived men's "ideal women" as significantly more passive and accepting of a subordinate role with respect to both their personality development and their place in the family.[6]

It seems fair to say that the initial and critical task for a woman who wishes to respect herself as a whole person and seriously consider her options in regard to career and/or marriage and children involves three steps: (1) identifying with a competent older woman or family member who treats her aspirations seriously; (2) respecting and identifying with women her own age who are similarly self-involved; and (3) working out a satisfactory relationship with a man who also takes her aspirations seriously and who respects and encourages her intellect, activity, and competitiveness without being threatened. The significant man may be a boy friend but he could just as well be a male faculty member, a therapist, or a counselor.

Relationship to other women. Keniston found in one study that women in the process of redefining their gender role assume that other women will probably make indifferent, boring, or inferior companions.[7]

> Only prolonged exposure to another woman who is obviously not any of these things could alter this presumption. With men, however, the presumption was generally favorable: Men were expected to be lively and interesting; men's conversation was about more serious topics; time spent with men was usually better spent than time spent with women.

Keniston feels that it would be a mistake to think these women are depreciating women as such, but perhaps correct to see them as "having sharply differentiated themselves from the majority of women and as assuming—perhaps correctly—that most women have not followed their pathway to development." [8]

Although Keniston's subjects may not be typical, it would not be surprising if a number of women shared their attitudes, considering some of the prevailing cultural stereotypes about women. The women he studied worked with mostly male colleagues, and in their private lives they were involved in confirming and consolidating their new relationships with men.

> Only in special groups like Women's Liberation consciousness-raising groups does intimate contact with other women occur. When

it does, some of the attitudes mentioned—e.g., the ambivalence and rejection of other women—tend to become more conscious and to be at least partly resolved. And only under these rather special circumstances are such young women likely to discover their deep bonds with each other.[9]

One aspect of women's relationships to each other that cannot be overlooked is the sexual. It is certainly conceivable that increased emphasis on the personal worth of women may lead to increasing numbers of homosexual attachments, both emotional and physical. Lesbianism has been an issue in some of the groups within the women's movement, but it is impossible to ascertain whether it has really increased or whether it is simply more openly discussed, in accord with the general openness of the Gay Liberation movement. It would not be surprising if lesbianism had become more common, in view of the current sentiment against further population expansion, the new approval of individual self-expression, and the stated opinion of some women that heterosexual marriage is a trap devised by men for their own benefit. Because a few prominent feminists have made public statements about their own homosexual or bisexual orientation, there has been considerable publicity on the subject, but it is as yet unclear how significant such behavior will be for the average woman.

Relationships with men.   Just as women who redefine their gender roles need other women like themselves with whom they can associate comfortably, they need men who are willing to question the stereotypes of the masculine role. Finding a man who is willing to re-examine some of his own traditional independent aggressiveness and competitiveness, perhaps forgo some of it, and allow the expression of similar qualities in a woman is surely one of the major tasks of the woman seeking autonomy. But perhaps there is hope. In another study, Steinmann administered the inventory of 122 pairs of opposite traits described in chapter six to 562 American college men.[10] Data from their questionnaires indicate that their "ideal women" are significantly more active and self-assertive than the ideal which the women of the earlier Steinmann study attributed to them. These studies were conducted in 1964 and 1966, and there is more recent impressionistic evidence that college men and women to an increasing extent are getting closer to each other and becoming more respectful of each other's efforts to change.

But when a woman's career aspirations place her in competition with men, there seems to be less change. The American psychologist Matina Horner notes evidence that even today highly intelligent women continue

. . . consciously or unconsciously [to] equate intellectual achievement with loss of femininity. A bright woman is caught in a double bind. In testing and other achievement-oriented situations she worries not only about failure but also about success. If she fails, she is not living up to her own standards of performance; if she succeeds, she is not living up to societal expectations about the female role. Men in our society do not experience this kind of ambivalence because they are not only permitted, but actively encouraged to do well. For women, then, the desire to achieve is often contaminated by the motive to avoid success.[11]

In Horner's test results, more than 65 per cent of the women, but fewer than 10 per cent of the men, showed evidence of "the motive to avoid success. . . . These findings suggest that most women will fully explore their intellectual potential only when they do not need to compete—and least of all, when they *are* competing with men." [12] One wonders if these women might not do better in an all-women college, but if so, they would possibly still have to meet the problem later on.

This was most true of women with a strong anxiety about success. Unfortunately, these are often the same women who could be very successful if they were free from that anxiety. The girls in [the] sample who feared success also tended to have high intellectual ability and histories of academic success. (It is interesting to note that all but two of these girls were majoring in the humanities and in spite of very high grade points, aspired to traditional female careers: housewife, mother, nurse, schoolteacher. Girls who did not fear success, however, were aspiring to graduate degrees and careers in such scientific areas as math, physics, and chemistry.)

We can see from this small study that achievement-motivation in women is much more complex than is the same drive in men. Most men do not find many inhibiting forces in their path if they are able and motivated to succeed. As a result, they are not threatened by competition; in fact, surpassing an opponent is a source of pride and enhanced masculinity.

In recent years many legal and educational barriers to female achievement have been removed; but it is clear that a psychological barrier remains. The motive to avoid success has an all too important influence on the intellectual and professional lives of women in our society. [13]

It is significant that "success" in this study was automatically assumed to be congruent with traditional masculine definitions of achievement.

Faced with these feelings about the consequences of academic or career success, women students deal in a variety of ways with the possibility of achievement in an intellectually competitive field. Some attempt to be "better men" and to perform as "one of the boys." Others unconsciously deny any difficulties, fail to perceive negative attitudes, and learn to appear passive, compliant, and uncompetitive. Still others create an image of confusion, of being scatterbrained, either deliberatively as a cover-up, or inadvertently as a result of conflicting internal self-images. A woman may feel that she has to choose between a "feminine" style, usually somewhat vague and scatterbrained, and one which is termed aggressive and "castrating."

Any career-oriented woman may have more than one disappointment in her search for men who can be flexible toward her career plans and her self-concept. She may begin to wonder whether the end is worth the pain and loneliness experienced in the process of reaching her goal. Keniston has found a high tolerance for feelings of conflict and uncertainty in women who, while building a career, continue to try to work out some nontraditional relationship with a man or are willing to accept the risk that no such relationship will ever materialize. He suggests that the capacity to endure this uncertainty may be a major factor in a woman's ability to stick to a career path.

As has been pointed out, no such dilemma exists for the man. For him a career is seen as a logical step preceding establishment of a permanent relationship with a woman—although the sequence may at times be changed. Conversely, for a woman, a career may be regarded as an unnecessary step that can complicate or prevent establishment of a permanent relationship with a man and the raising of a family. Both these goals remain important, despite recent changes in attitude among college women suggesting that a career is considered equally important.[14] Clearly these continuing disparities between attitudes expressed by men and women interfere with the development of satisfactory new balances in relationships between the sexes.

IN MEN'S ROLES

Thus far discussion has centered almost exclusively on women, although much that has been said applies to men as well. Women have been more neglected than men in our institutions of higher learning, which on the whole have acted as though there were only one sex in college. But men have been constrained in their own way. As with women, models for changed male roles are not readily available. To give up the stereotype of independent, aggressive competitiveness without being deprecated as "feminine" by oneself, other men, women, or society in general is a task that confronts men just as exquisitely as comparable tasks confront women.

The price men appear to have paid for following the stereotypes of competitiveness and aggressiveness, along with the concomitant goals of success and achievement, has been high. The study of psychosomatic medicine reveals that many forms of psychosomatic illness, regardless of cause, occur more frequently in men than in women, particularly in men who do not accept their own needs to be dependent. There is a much higher incidence in men of cardiovascular diseases such as stroke, coronary occlusion, and hypertension. In part, current theory relates this to men's feeling that they must be aggressive and hard-driving in order to maintain a satisfactory masculine self-image. It remains to be seen whether role changes now taking place will affect the incidence and age of onset of such illnesses in women.

There are indications of important changes in men's attitudes. In a recent study of college students,[15] male respondents approved of women's pursuing careers for the sake of their own development. Furthermore, men are now generally willing to accept the idea that women will earn some of the family money, even though many, but by no means all, men continue to see themselves as the primary breadwinners. Finally, more than 60 per cent of both men and women students in the study cited agreed that participation in child-rearing should be about equal. It appears that some men are beginning to visualize themselves as undertaking tasks previously considered "feminine," and presumably when family tasks are more evenly divided, the rat race of business or professional life may become less than all-engulfing.

As men change the concept of their gender role, they may also look for women with qualities and goals that are different from those traditionally thought of as desirable. It is easier to express such attitudes verbally, however, than it is to put them into practice. One cannot always know what one's reactions will be when the demands of a family actually occur.

In Marital Relationships

The relatively new concept of "egalitarian marriage," which is related to that of the two-career family, is a natural outgrowth of the movement for equality for women. In the past, husband and wife have filled clear-cut complementary roles in the marriage. These roles have varied in different societies and in different social groups. Although practice may often have deviated from theory, the cultural ideal has always been unmistakable. Depending on social class and particular viewpoint, there have been differences of opinion as to who had the best of the bargain, but there was no question that there was a bargain in the sense of a trade. Neither partner was expected to stray very far from the agreed-upon role. Generally, in our society, the woman has been responsible for food preparation, child care, home care, and the selection of household fixtures and clothing; the man has been responsible for economic support, the heavy home tasks, the purchase of major household items, and often family "business" matters. Over the years, however, this model has been questioned, and the recent feminist movement has strongly protested the concept and its consequences. If the educated woman is going to have the opportunity to use her training in any sort of career, modifications are essential.

An alternate suggestion is the egalitarian marriage, in which each partner has equal opportunity and is not automatically assigned to a particular role or task. This is a laudable ideal, but one that in practice clearly requires considerable ingenuity, flexibility, and good will from both partners if it is to work. For any two people living together, a minimum of tasks must be done so that life can run smoothly and when children are added this minimum significantly increases and the tasks themselves become more complex.

The area in which equality can be established most unequivocally is that of outside occupation. When both partners have careers, however, it is possible to visualize situations in which the interests of one might come into conflict with the interests of the other. Recently several researchers, notably the Rapoports[16] and Lynda Holmstrom,[17] have studied the two-career family and have drawn some conclusions as to how couples have satisfactorily worked out the problems involved.

In a study on couples with children, the Rapoports conclude that the essential adaptation is "a division of labor in relation to family functions that is distributed between the partners on an equal-style basis." Various household and family tasks were divided by "skills and inclinations present in the specific partnership" rather than by traditional gender-role determinations. All couples, however, were dependent on the availability of some domestic help and had to assign priorities for child care, house care, and leisure and social activities.

Some of the couples studied were inclined to choose, when possible, jobs that did not spill over into nonworking periods, and they stressed the importance of a rather careful organization of necessary tasks so that the more important tasks (such as child care) would not be neglected as a result of time consumed by less significant activities. The Rapoports also observed lines of tension between partners which were handled in a variety of ways by different couples. Sometimes a partner (more often the wife) adopted a different "personality" at work from the one she had at home; in some cases a clear-cut opportunity for one partner was sacrificed because there was no acceptable opportunity for the other; and there were transient periods for some couples when one partner shouldered more of the household activities than the other.

The Rapoports developed a cost-benefit scheme of evaluation and applied it to five technically defined areas of stress.[18] In general, couples seemed to work out solutions by establishing lines of demarcation for all activities, within which they felt they could comfortably function as separate and distinct individuals. At times it was necessary to work out efficiency procedures different from customary practice, which sometimes resulted in guilt feelings and often led to resentment and criticism from friends and relatives—a consequence which presumably will become rarer as the two-career family becomes more prevalent. The investigators point out that different periods within the marriage may place the highest strain on one or another aspect of family functioning, and it is their opinion that accommodation to these strains is essential to family balance. They stress the need for flexibility on the part of both the partners *and* the society.

In a similar study, Holmstrom described four barriers to success of the two-career marriage: (1) the pressure to move geographically for career advancement; (2) the definition of *career* as an all-consuming activity; (3) the concept of the wife as an auxiliary to the husband's career (for instance, as hostess); and (4) the difficulty of raising children in the isolated nuclear family.[19] In her study, the issue of geography arose among 75 per cent of the respondent couples, and in every case the wife's career had been affected by the husband's move. Surprisingly, in many cases the wife's career also affected, at least once, the decision as to where to live, although the husband was the determining factor in family relocation more often than the wife. With regard to the other three barriers, concerted effort and often considerable adaptation were required to overcome them. For example, time became particularly scarce, and highly efficient schedules had to be devised for both partners. Holmstrom feels that society should make greater adaptations to help solve the problems she found among these couples.

American psychologist Paul Rosenkrantz conducted a study on egalitarian families and found as an immediate difficulty the lack of suitable models.[20] He also concluded that when the family has children, gender-role conflicts are much more in evidence because "there is just much more work when children arrive." One characteristic of the couples he studied was an open display of and tolerance for conflict. He found that the working through of these conflicts, where successful, seemed to strengthen the union. The couples studied placed a high value on intimacy, and he points out that they did not eliminate dependency but rather developed greater adaptability—that is, they had "a more flexible choice of appropriate ways of expressing . . . dependency needs, of differentiating appropriate circumstances and appropriate people on whom to be dependent."

Children put a particular strain on this kind of marriage, and, whether in anticipation of this problem or in increasing awareness of the need for population control, more people than before now contemplate marriage without children. A recent study indicated that 10 to 15 per cent of students polled did not want children. From the Depression until very recently the pressure to procreate has been strong, and it is safe to say that most couples married during this period with the expectation that they would have at least one child. It is difficult to know how many of those who did not have children remained childless out of choice, but their number is probably relatively small. As has been mentioned, with the development of satisfactory, reasonably foolproof methods of contraception, the choice not to reproduce is now open to every couple, and simultaneously efforts toward population control have for the first time placed a positive social value on nonprocreation. A couple today can consider their own feelings about having a child and make a deliberate decision against doing so, thus unquestionably lightening the burdens of family maintenance and lessening the conflicts between career and home responsibilities. In particular a childless marriage demands less of a woman and eliminates the sharp conflict between child-care responsibilities during the early years and heavy work obligations at a crucial period in the establishment of her career. As with so many choices, however, the decision may be determined more by unconscious feelings than by conscious planning.

Even if children are desired by the two-career couple, limiting their number and spacing their arrival may reduce the time and energy necessary for child care at any given period. At one time the one-child family was not considered a good environment for the child, but recent studies seem to have contradicted this belief. Many families now feel that two is the ideal number of children; a generation ago four or five were frequently desired and produced. But children satisfy many unconscious needs, and the current rationale for small families may be superseded by another rationale which reverses the trend.

The concept of equality in marriage has been an important new development in the United States, but it is still so novel that one can do little more than cite the problems encountered and the empirical solutions so far attempted. In any event, the two-career family calls for considerable flexibility in the partners, whose adjustment could be greatly aided by more flexibility on the part of society.

In Living Patterns

Some possible changes in permanent patterns of living have been touched on. Currently, however, more revolutionary breaks with past living arrangements are being proposed, among which are open marriage, communal living, homosexual marriage, and the single state.

Open marriage. This concept in a certain sense embodies an attempt to respond to the increase in human longevity and the great reduction in time that must be devoted to child-rearing. Marriage today may have several distinct phases, during which the needs of the partners change significantly. As defined by the American anthropologists Nena and George O'Neill, open marriage involves revision of many of the standard conventions.[21] For the O'Neills, it does not necessarily imply extramarital sexual relationships, although it does not rule them out, either. It presumably allows the woman greater flexibility in the pursuit of a career because it diminishes the expectation that each partner will carry out preordained roles. Such events as separation of the partners because of career requirements, or transitory relationships with others, are regarded as part of the expectable pattern of the marriage rather than as evidence of marital tension. How well this concept of marriage works in practice is not yet clear.

Communal living. This has been a rather conspicuous pattern of living in the past few years. In many communes, the group is held together by common interests or by one guiding principle, such as a set of religious beliefs or rejection of urban living and an active participation in farm life. Theoretically, communal living duplicates the "extended family" in the period preceding World War I, although factually the extended family was never a widespread feature of American society. Communes facilitate a sharing of child-rearing tasks and housekeeping chores that allows a woman with a baby to work outside the home relieved of the need to make elaborate and often unreliable baby-sitting arrangements. Theoretically the existence of "multiple mothers" may decrease the dependence of the child on the biological mother, and eliminate possible psychological harm to the child from the absence of the mother. The *kibbutzim* of Israel, although initially developed for a somewhat different reason, have unquestionably provided a model for and influenced the development of communal living.

Homosexual marriage. Although this arrangement has probably existed informally and clandestinely for some time, it has only recently emerged on the current social horizon as an alternate living style. Its public debut is in part related to the recent emergence of the Gay Liberation movement, which, in addition to protesting general social discrimination against homosexually oriented individuals, has called attention to the inequities of tax laws, adoption laws, and some housing codes. The idea of homosexual marriage appeals to women who feel that true independence for them means the exclusion of any significant relationships with men. Obviously, these marriages have the same potential problems of dominance, division of labor, priority of careers, and so on, as do heterosexual marriages. Nevertheless, some women feel that these problems become very different when male and female gender roles are not involved and the weight of tradition does not burden the relationship with guilt or resentment.

The single state. Not all women in the past have married, although one might deduce from reading about single women that those who have remained single have not done so out of choice. Actually, there is some evidence to suggest that women in the early part of the century who chose serious careers at least harbored a subliminal awareness and acceptance of the possibility that they might not marry. What is not clear is whether they elected to remain single in order to be able to continue with their work; whether they saw marriage and career as incompatible, and, perhaps reluctantly, chose the latter; whether their competence made them frightening to men, so that relationships with men did not develop; or whether their earning power made it unnecessary for them to accept a less-than-ideal proposal of marriage merely for economic security.

It should be noted that many women have developed significant careers after becoming widows; it seems that, at least in the past, single women had careers much more often than did married ones.

In any event, because of the social mores of the early part of the century, being single meant giving up sexual relations. Some women may have managed liaisons, but they obviously were hazardous and could rarely be acknowledged without risking scandal. Today, however, there is a more permissive attitude toward sexual activity outside marriage, and a woman can elect to remain single and still maintain an active sexual life. She can even bear (or with some difficulty adopt) and raise a child without evoking the social opprobrium that would have greeted her even a generation ago. For some women unmarried motherhood has attractions because it sidesteps conflicts over job priorities, geographic location of the family, and even the necessity for establishing marital division of labor, but it exacerbates the demands of child care because there is no husband with whom to share the responsibility.

It is too soon to assess the long-range effects of any of these patterns for living. It is possible to see advantages and disadvantages in all of them, and it is safe to say that not everyone could adapt to each pattern. Furthermore, it would be naïve to assume that these patterns are totally acceptable today, any more than they would have been a decade ago. In fact, there is considerable evidence that many adults continue to disapprove of homosexual behavior and of both premarital and extramarital sexual activity, so that a woman electing one or another of these patterns still may expect social disapproval.[22] But in one study on campus only 10 per cent of college students disapproved of premarital sex, indicating either that attitudes are changing or that younger population groups have values significantly different from those of their elders.[23]

Probably the main reason for scrutinizing these patterns is that they challenge many of our unconsciously held assumptions and thus may serve to hold up a mirror to conventional living patterns. If the homosexual pair can work out harmonious patterns of joint living that do not automatically make assumptions about gender role or dominance and submission, it is only logical to ask why a heterosexual pair cannot do the same. Indeed, recognition of the very existence of different living patterns shows that the needs and preferences of people differ and that resistance to conformity should be encouraged rather than condemned.

In Institutions

It is not easy to forecast the changes that may occur in institutional patterns, and it is clear that some of them can take place only gradually over a period of time. The importance of models for women college students has been suggested, but it will take time before women in large numbers will be available as candidates for faculty, business, and professional positions because at the moment relatively few have gone through the necessary preparatory steps.[24] For this reason, colleges should encourage women prepared for and interested in such posts, rather than blocking them with rigid policies that were designed for different purposes in an era now past.

One example of such policies is the so-called nepotism policy that existed (or exists) in many colleges. Actually this is usually an "anti-nepotism" regulation that prohibits the employment of both husband and wife by the college or department within the college. It is doubtful that its original purpose was to prevent women from progressing in careers. Presumably it was designed to prevent special privilege from accruing to one member of the couple as a result of influence by the other, and to avoid situations in which action taken in relation to one partner might create difficulty or embarrassment for the spouse. In effect, however, it has operated to prevent both partners in a couple from working in perhaps the only appropriate jobs available in a given geographical area. Since the man's career has usually been the determining factor in the choice of family location, a "nepotism policy" meant that the woman was forced to travel long distances to a suitable job, work at a job on a lower level, or give up all pretense of a career. Elimination of "nepotism policies" where they still exist is clearly called for.

Other overdue institutional changes concern greater flexibility in leave policies, more part-time opportunities, and work schedules that consider the child-care responsibilities of qualified candidates. Frequently these are not easy to work out, but institutions really interested in encouraging women to assume a larger share of the job opportunities available must give the same careful thought to the enforcement of these changes that a commercial enterprise gives to improving its profit margins. There is a long-standing tradition of granting employees a certain number of sick-leave days a year. This practice could be extended to apply to caring for the sick. Working women should be able to take time off to care for a sick child without feeling that they are doing something untoward. If a similar policy were established for men, care of the sick could be shared and the issue of who in the family was sick would be less important than that care was provided in answer to an employee's genuine need.

Maternity and paternity leave is a conspicuous example of an important change that has been made in some organizations. The use of part-time employees is another. One of the problems of part-time employment is that the worker often feels isolated from the mainstream of activities—more of a "piece worker" than anything else. Employers might attempt to relate their part-time workers to the functioning of the total organization. One suggested method adapts the "partnership principle," whereby a given job (suited to such treatment) is split between two workers, who share the responsibility for information exchange, much as nurses or doctors pass on orders and reports from the outgoing shift to the incoming shift.

Child care poses particularly difficult problems for a variety of reasons, but there can be new solutions. Some of the difficulty comes from the conflict already noted—that is, between the peak demand for child care, which occurs early in most people's careers, and a concurrent demand for especially hard work in the process of establishing oneself in one's chosen field. Day care is frequently suggested as an answer, but it does not settle all the difficulties involved. There seems to be no solution to this problem that is entirely satisfactory.

Another current problem in American colleges concerns the shortage of qualified women teachers and the effect on women of the tenure system. The attempt to represent women adequately on various policy-making committees inevitably cuts into the time available to women to further their own scholarship. Yet when tenure is in question, they will suffer if scholarship has been neglected. They are caught between the immediate demand for input into the policy-making apparatus and the demand for career advancement, which in the long run may provide them with greater opportunities for leadership. Presumably this dilemma will be resolved by the employment of greater numbers of women. But its persistence only underlines the need for more advancement opportunities for women.

Colleges have been urged to offer curriculum courses that focus on women's contribution to all spheres of life. Many colleges have responded by adding a special course to an established department; others have initiated a major in Women's Studies. The particular method of incorporating such studies in the curriculum is less important than the recognition that women have assayed and succeeded in a variety of roles, many of which call for traits and talents very different from the stereotyped "feminine" attributes.

Besides the adjustments just discussed, a different kind of learning might be explored. To gain a real grasp of the issues, both women and men students need to be directly exposed to various occupations and life styles. The American anthropologist Margaret Mead has suggested that women undergraduates be provided with internships in families. If this suggestion is followed, similar internships should certainly also be provided for men. American college students who have been attached to foreign families as part of their education have enlarged their attitudes and expanded their knowledge of variations in family life. The term *internship* may be too pretentious, but some such exposure in depth to another way of living seems to have particular merit during this current transitional period when new possibilities in styles of living are being explored.

The observations, research, or internships envisaged here might all be linked to traditional classroom learning, which could only benefit from the process. But observation and research in themselves offer limited experiences for learning, and undergraduates might be involved personally in experiment and innovation. For example, they might begin by studying a particular business organization or city government, assess the roles assigned to women in the structure under study, and then proceed to make recommendations for better utilization of women by the creation of new roles or even new occupations. Such a study would be incomplete without follow-up observations on what happens as a result of their recommendations. This is action research, a much-needed style of learning. Similar projects could be related specifically to theories of child-rearing and linked directly to child-study programs already in existence at many colleges.

These suggestions imply an enlargement of the college's function in two ways: (1) undergraduate work would become more closely related than at present to the problems of society and their solutions; and (2) the total development of the person would become a deliberate focus of attention. College might thus provide the incentive for real development of awareness, now so often lacking, by relating intellectual activity directly to aspects of the student's own life.

On a more mundane level, colleges must provide the same adjunct facilities for women that they provide for men, whether in athletics, in health, or in career counseling, and these facilities must take into account the differences between men and women.

Although there are times when policies, laws, services, or attitudes can be appropriately gender-blind, women have some special needs—for example, gynecological services. Similarly, some differences will occur in athletic preferences and needs and in career advising, which still must accommodate to the fact that, if a child is to be born, it will be carried and delivered by the woman. Sex counseling is desirable for both sexes, but special counseling may be required for women's contraceptive methods. The college psychiatrist can help both men and women through individual counseling and by advising faculty and administration on policies that may alter restrictive attitudes toward women and increase the number of options open to them. Colleges can also experiment with housing alternatives, which may enhance women's confidence in themselves, as one study of co-residency has recently suggested.[25]

Finally, there must be some institutions that will attempt to vary quite radically the patterns of education. Recently Barbara Newell, president of Wellesley College in Massachusetts, spoke about offering admission to a significant number of women in the middle years, women whose childbearing and child-rearing years were behind them. A few colleges and professional "schools without walls" have been established with the objective of making attendance more possible for, although not limited to, women who have time to study but find it difficult to leave home on a regularly scheduled basis. Perhaps an upgrading of correspondence courses could be attempted with a similar student body in mind. In this connection, the rapid development of cable television could provide the vehicle for classroom instruction and at the same time make possible the collection of tuition fees. Such measures will be effective, however, only if they are of high quality and avoid the image of being "for women," which often implies "second-rate."

CHANGES IN SOCIAL VALUES

The prospect of radical and rapid change of social values in a society as complex as that of the United States is perhaps an illusion. Yet it is necessary to stress that men have clearly been the dominant sex and that therefore their values have been dominant. Historically, feminist movements have striven for the goal of equality (equal suffrage, equal job opportunity, equal pay, and so forth) and, understandably, have tended to accept male values and to assume that, if women are to take advantage of equal career opportunities, they will have to display the same aggressiveness, competitiveness and sometimes ruthlessness of their male colleagues.

A more far-reaching social change would be a shift in the system of values of the whole society, so that it would not necessarily reward these particular qualities but would also favor traditionally "feminine" qualities of cooperation, sensitivity, and finesse. Even the concept of success might be redefined so that power and money and status were not necessarily the yardsticks by which achievement is measured, but rather service and excellence of performance for its own sake.

In the pursuit of quality it is essential that many current administrative practices in organizations, both private and public, be changed to eliminate discrimination against women. Tax laws, insurance regulations and credit policies all currently distinguish between men and women and, almost without exception, favor men in so doing. Such discrimination, while perhaps not central to the woman's dilemma, inevitably creates frustration, enhances feelings of low self-esteem, and significantly interferes with a woman's freedom of action.

eight CONCLUSIONS AND
RECOMMENDATIONS

This book outlines the very real problems facing the college woman—and man—in universities and in society today. It examines some of the influences that shape the internal attitudes of women, some of the external factors that impinge on their choices, and the consequences of these choices. It identifies attitudes, practices, and policies that we believe should be changed by policy-making members of the university and the society, including mental health professionals. The most difficult task has been to describe these changes and how they could be made. Colleges vary greatly and they and the society of which they are a part inevitably change both attitudes and practice slowly. Nevertheless, recognition of the problem is an essential first step, and a willingness to consider change is the crucial next step, if change is to occur.

There are six major changes that seem essential for the well-being and progress of women in college and afterward, three

146

in the sphere of personal relationships and three in the institutional sphere:

(1) A more open definition of *femininity* and *masculinity*

(2) An emphasis on individual autonomy rather than adaptation to sex-role stereotypes as a definition of maturity

(3) An acceptance of variations in traditional male-female relationships, marital patterns, and child-rearing practices, with a reflection of this acceptance spelled out in institutional attitudes and practices

(4) An increased flexibility in both faculty and student arrangements for women

(5) An increase in the number of women appointed to prominent university positions, to act as role models and to share their experience with college women (and men)

(6) An attitude of "increased possibility" for women to participate significantly in all fields

A more open definition of femininity and masculinity. The traditional definition of femininity involves passivity, submissiveness, intuitiveness and sensitivity, and, as a corollary, the avoidance of aggressiveness, competitiveness, rationality, and logical thinking. If she adheres to this definition, a woman, no matter how educated, is at an almost insurmountable disadvantage in the pursuit of a career. If the college or the society is serious about encouraging women to undertake roles other than those of housewife and mother, this traditional definition must be modified. Although these "feminine" qualities are traditionally associated with the capacity for motherhood and wifehood, when scrutinized they do not really fit the woman for even those roles. Anyone who has attempted to run a household knows that many of the "nonfeminine" qualities are essential to success in domestic affairs as well as in a profession or a business. But when these qualities are exercised in the traditionally masculine world, they suddenly take on a different implication for both men and women. The woman who speaks up in the man's sphere is labeled "aggressive," a term with a particularly pejorative connotation when applied to women.

As the concept of femininity is modified, the traditional definition of masculinity will inevitably be modified also. Many of the adjectives used to signify "feminine" require another person to complete their meaning, and that other person is a man. The attribute of submissiveness implies submissiveness to a man, not to a woman (although a woman who is dominant in relation to other women may be described as "a masculine woman"), and it requires dominance from the man to complete the dyad. Similarly, *competitiveness* often implies competition with a man. To a great extent the pressure for women to be "feminine" simply dictates that they be feminine in their relation to men, who supposedly see a threat to their "masculinity" if there is any shift in the balance of the traditional male-female relationship. If men could be less rigid in their definition of masculinity, and if they could accept the fact that they do not have to display traditional "masculine" qualities in every situation, a greater range of behavior, without anxiety on the part of either sex, would become possible.

An emphasis on individual autonomy. The most significant contribution of psychiatry to human growth and development has been the encouragement of ego autonomy. Ego autonomy is a highly complex concept that defies simple definition, but, roughly, it means that a person is able to control his or her life by adaptive choice and independent action. With ego autonomy one has the inner freedom to develop one's potential both emotionally and intellectually. It implies the capacity to acknowledge reality in the process of making choices, but does *not* mean simply "adjusting" to the status quo or to a specific social milieu. Ego autonomy calls for the ability to accept interdependence with other individuals and in the process to benefit from these dependencies rather than be crippled by them. There are inevitably differences in definitions of ego autonomy, and the most abstract definition is a rather Utopian one, but it can serve as a guide in avoiding some of the pitfalls involved in oversimplifying the concept.

The one principle to be observed above all others is that the individuality of every person is valuable and should be defended when it is attacked by pressures for conformity. This is not to endorse simply "doing your own thing" but to stress the options available during any person's development, especially with regard to young women, who are particularly burdened by the excess baggage of rigid institutional and societal expectations.

Acceptance of variations in male-female relationships and child-rearing practices. Two-career families, egalitarian marriages, and partial or complete reversal of the roles of parents are relatively new concepts in family living that are being tried by couples today. Although it is too soon to tell whether they will survive, it is imperative to be open to such experiments in order to further the realization of the first two recommendations given here. Many couples will prefer the traditional male-female role relationship in marriage, and the recommendation for openness in this book does not militate against that pattern. The woman who finds fulfillment in the role of wife and mother—and there are many—should not be forced into another pattern in order to conform to feminist ideology. To believe that one *must* combine marriage and career is just as limiting as to believe that one must be solely a homemaker. The woman who sees homemaking as only a partial means to self-realization, or who sees it as a temporary part of a broader life plan, may require a different marital pattern, and it is to these women, who currently have few guideposts, that much of this book is addressed. Furthermore, there may be both women and men who eschew formal marriage and work out satisfactory relationships while remaining single.

In regard to child-rearing, in the last century every advance in medicine and psychology has inspired another authoritative formula for raising children. But at present there is much less certainty—or at least agreement—about the "right" way of raising children. Approaches are more varied, partly as a consequence of disillusion with the authorities of the past and partly in response to the changing needs and goals of individual parents. Further research should be directed toward observing the results of these variations.

Increased flexibility in faculty and student arrangements. There are women who manage full-time careers without serious conflict. Some choose to forgo marriage and family. Others have the energy and resources to combine family and career successfully. Whichever path women choose, they confront conflicts which men do not. Today's college students are trying to work out patterns of study, life, and work that will enable both men and women to assume family responsibilities and at the same time follow long-range careers. They are questioning the intense competitiveness, the "success syndrome," and the more than sixty hours a week taken for granted in many occupations. In trying to work out new patterns, they encounter inflexible institutional policies and structures that present formidable barriers. Frequently part-time work or study opportunities are either unavailable or available only at a sacrifice of quality. Child-care resources are either inadequate or lacking altogether. Many regulations are specifically designed to discourage interruptions in curriculum.

In many other ways colleges have not adapted to the fact that students may be married and already have family concerns. Counseling services are needed to help young men and women cope with changing family roles because such changes pose real problems for both sexes. It can be argued that students "don't have to get married," but the fact is that many do marry, and in a society that values individual freedom of choice, the institutions must recognize that policies adequate in the past no longer meet today's needs and will certainly not be appropriate for the future. Much trauma for individuals, for families, and for children yet to be born will result if institutions adhere rigidly to tradition instead of finding ways to make institutional goals compatible with the rapidly changing social patterns.

Increased flexibility and a greater variety of options will undoubtedly benefit men as well as women, although the most urgent pressure is unquestionably felt by women.

An increase in the number of women appointed to university positions. Since women holding prominent faculty and administrative positions, who could serve as models, are rare, women students find it difficult to see themselves in the future in a career, or to believe they will find career opportunities after they develop specific interests. The absence of such models also handicaps men, who would have the opportunity to observe women as colleagues, not just as mothers or wives.

In our culture there is a general expectation that family matters affect career plans for both women and men. This creates special stresses and problems for women students, and there is a considerable loss to the professions when talented women do not embark on training or do not complete their training because of the barriers they encounter along the way. In most colleges little thought is given to working out a flexible program for the student, woman or man.

In view of the way girls are raised, it is perhaps not surprising that many women accept this situation as a *fait accompli* and express little anger about it. Their reaction is probably a continuation of the adaptive process developed earlier in life as a means of getting along in school. But the anger is frequently present and often erupts later after the full impact of the deprivation has been felt. Hence the woman student needs counseling services, women friends with common interests, and role models, especially in schools with few women students, women faculty members, or women administrators. Until re-

cently, women felt that they should receive no special considera-
tion because of their sex and did not particularly value communication with other women. With the increase of feminist activity,
many women are discovering the importance of providing
support for one another and the benefits of obtaining information
from women who have found different solutions for a common
problem.

An increased possibility for women to participate in all fields.
Both college and society must genuinely believe that it is
becoming increasingly possible for women to attempt and to
succeed in any role. There have been some attempts recently to
help women to feel that they can enter any field, but old attitudes
die hard, and many prejudices come to the surface when a woman
does inquire about entering a hitherto male-dominated field.
Although there have been occasional women surgeons for
decades, a career in surgery for a woman is still considered
sufficiently unusual that she is often discouraged from preparing
for it. Such discouragement may take the form of a "realistic"
description, usually by a male, of the difficulties of a career in that
field. This would be reasonable enough, except for the fact that
the majority of difficulties cited apply equally to men, but men
are expected to be able to deal with adversity as part of their
working life, whereas women are to be "protected."

Sometimes discouragement takes the cruder form of describing
the hostility the woman will meet, which presumably will
interfere with eventual success. A more subtle form of this
approach is the question, "Why subject yourself to so much
unpleasantness when you don't have to?" Indeed, this is a
particularly difficult argument to counter because it encompasses

some truth. Many, if not all, careers involve work that is either boring or unpleasant or both, and it is reasonable to avoid such work where possible. The argument omits to mention, however, both the gratifications that may derive from a career and the potential "unpleasantness" involved in the alternative to a career.

These attitudes are also expressed gratuitously in college in a myriad of ways. Sometimes the college president refers to "our beautiful coeds," thereby suggesting that beauty is their major contribution to college life. More important, career counseling offices have been organized primarily to advise male students on their way to business or industry. Obviously, it is not appropriate for the college to recruit women to fields in which they have no interest, but it is essential that when interest is expressed it be encouraged to the same extent that a similar interest by a man would be encouraged.

The college woman of today faces a future marked by uncertainty, difficulty, and probably some frustration—but one that also offers a hitherto nonexistent range of options and possibilities. Excitement, opportunity, and creativity are available to her, but she must contend with external inflexibility, reaction, and at times naked hostility, as well as with internal obstacles grounded in her own learned responses about what it means to be a woman. The one experience that she is certain to meet is conflict. But it is perhaps only slightly overoptimistic to believe that through conflict can come growth. All women will not find Utopian solutions. Some may be miserable, and for many the availability of choice only adds a burden. Nevertheless, the changes that have begun in the last few years hold forth real hope to women that they will be able to use their education creatively. And these changes can lead to greater fulfillment for a greater number of women than ever before and, as a corollary, should also enhance the fulfillment of men.

REFERENCE NOTES

FOR FURTHER READING

INDEX

REFERENCE NOTES

one INTRODUCTION

1. Jane O'Reilly, "The View from My Bed," *Ms.*, April 1973.
2. Philip Goldberg, "Are Women Prejudiced against Women?" *Trans-action*, 5: 28–30 (1968).

two A HISTORICAL PERSPECTIVE

1. Alice S. Rossi, "Equality between the Sexes: An Immodest Proposal," in *The Woman in America*, ed. Robert J. Lifton (Boston: Beacon Press, 1967), pp. 98–143.
2. John Demos, "Myth and Reality in the History of American Family Life," in *Marriage Problems and Prospects*, ed. Henry Grunebaum & Jacob Christ (Boston: Little, Brown, 1974).
3. Carl N. Degler, "Revolution without Ideology: The Changing Place of Women in America," in *The Woman in America* (Boston: Beacon Press, 1967), pp. 193–210.

4. John Demos, *op. cit.*
5. *Encyclopaedia Britannica* (Chicago: William Benton, 1963), Vol. 23, pp. 702ff.
6. *Ibid.*
7. E. James Lieberman, "American Families and the Vietnam War," *Journal of Marriage & the Family* 33: 709–722 (1971).
8. Carl N. Degler, *op. cit.*
9. Thomas C. Mendenhall, "The Report of the President, 1971–1972," *Smith College Bulletin*, Series 67, No. III (May 1973).
10. Richard B. Morris (ed.), *Encyclopedia of American History* (New York: Harper & Brothers, 1953).
11. Connie Brown and Jane Seitz, "You've Come a Long Way, Baby: Historical Perspectives," in *Sisterhood is Powerful*, ed. Robin Morgan (New York: Random House, 1970), pp. 3–30.
12. William Acton, *The Functions and Disorders of the Reproductive Organs* (Philadelphia: Lindsay & Blakiston, 1867).
13. Sigmund Freud, "The Aetiology of Hysteria" (1896), in *Collected Papers* (New York: Basic Books, 1960), Vol. 1, pp. 183–219.
14. Margaret Sanger, *An Autobiography* (New York: W. W. Norton, 1938).
15. Ben Lindsey, *Companionate Marriage* (New York: Boni & Liveright, 1927).
16. Bertrand Russell, *Marriage and Morals* (New York: Bantam Books, 1968).
17. Cynthia Fuchs Epstein, *Woman's Place* (Berkeley, California: University of California Press, 1971).
18. Rossi, *op. cit.*
19. René Spitz and W. Godfrey Cobliner, *First Year of Life: A Psychoanalytic Study of Normal and Deviant Development of Object Relations* (New York: International Universities Press, 1966). John Bowlby, *Attachment* (New York: Basic Books, 1969).
20. Esther Peterson, "Working Women," in *The Woman in America* (Boston: Beacon Press, 1967), pp. 144–172.
21. Simone de Beauvoir, *The Second Sex* (New York: Bantam Books, 1963).
22. President's Commission on the Status of Women, *American*

Women: Report of the President's Commission (Washington, D. C.: Government Printing Office, 1963).
23. Betty Friedan, *The Feminine Mystique* (New York: Dell Publishing, 1963).
24. "The Woman in America," *Daedalus* 93, 2 (Spring 1964); also available as *The Woman in America* (Boston: Beacon Press, 1967).
25. Kate Millett, *Sexual Politics* (New York: Avon Books, 1971).
26. William H. Masters and Virginia E. Johnson, *Human Sexual Response* (Boston: Little, Brown, 1966).

three EXPECTATIONS OF WOMEN IN COLLEGE

1. U. S. Bureau of the Census, *Occupation by Industry* (Washington, D.C.: Government Printing Office, 1970), No. PC-7C, 1970.
2. *Women Today*, 3, 6 (March 19, 1973).
3. U. S. Department of Labor, Wage and Standards Administration, Women's Bureau, *Trends in Educational Attainment of Women* (Washington, D. C.: Government Printing Office, 1967).
4. Helen W. Astin, *The Woman Doctorate in America* (New York: Russell Sage Foundation, 1969).
5. *Wall Street Journal*, March 15, 1972, p. 3.
6. Juanita Kreps, *Sex in the Marketplace: American Women at Work* (Baltimore: Johns Hopkins University Press, 1971).
7. Group for the Advancement of Psychiatry, *Sex and the College Student*, Report No. 60 (New York: GAP, 1965).
8. Alexander Astin *et al., The American Freshman: National Norms for Fall 1973* (Washington, D.C.: American Council of Education, University of California at Los Angeles, 1974).
9. Jeanne H. Block, "Conceptions of Sex Role: Some Cross-Cultural and Longitudinal Perspectives," *American Psychologist*, 28: 512–526 (1973).
10. *Ibid.*

four THE FEMININE–MASCULINE AXIS

1. *Webster's New International Dictionary*, Second Edition, unabridged (Springfield, Massachusetts: G. & C. Merriam, 1947).
2. John Money, "Hermaphroditism," in *The Encyclopedia of Sexual Behavior*, ed. Albert Ellis & Albert Abarbanel (New York: Hawthorn Books, 1961), Vol. 1, pp. 472–484.
3. *Webster, op. cit.*
4. John Money and Anke A. Ehrhardt, *Man and Woman, Boy and Girl* (Baltimore: Johns Hopkins University Press, 1972).
5. Margaret Mead, *Sex and Temperament in Three Primitive Societies* (New York: William Morrow, 1935).
6. Warren J. Gadpaille, "Research into the Physiology of Maleness and Femaleness," *AMA Archives of General Psychiatry*, 26: 193–206 (1972).
7. *Ibid.*
8. Leonore Tiefer, "Commentary on 'Innate Masculine–Feminine Differences,'" *Medical Aspects of Human Sexuality*, 7: 156–157 (1973).
9. Robert J. Stoller, "Overview: The Impact of New Advances in Sex Research on Psychoanalytic Theory," *American Journal of Psychiatry*, 130: 241–251 (1973).
10. Margaret S. Mahler and Manuel Furer, "Certain Aspects of the Separation-Individuation Phase," *Psychoanalytic Quarterly*, 32: 1–14 (1963).
11. Willie Hoffer, "Development of the Body Ego," *Psychoanalytic Study of the Child*, 5: 18–23 (1950).
12. W. G. Joffe, "A Critical Review of the Status of the Envy Concept," *International Journal of Psychoanalysis*, 50: 533–545 (1969).
13. Roy Schafer, *Aspects of Internalization* (New York: International Universities Press, 1968).
14. Ralph R. Greenson, "Dis-Identifying from Mother: Its Special Importance for the Boy," *International Journal of Psychoanalysis*, 49: 370–374 (1968).
15. M. Leonard, "Fathers and Daughters," *International Journal of Psychoanalysis*, 47: 325–334 (1966).

16. Joseph Sandler, Alex Holder, and Dale Meers, "The Ego Ideal and the Ideal Self," *Psychoanalytic Study of the Child*, 18: 139–159 (1963).
17. Alfred C. Kinsey, Wardell B. Pomeroy, Clyde E. Martin, and Paul H. Gebhard, *Sexual Behavior in the Human Male* (Philadelphia: Saunders, 1948).
18. William H. Masters and Virginia E. Johnson, *Human Sexual Response* (Boston: Little, Brown, 1966).
19. Lester A. Kirkendall, "Sex Drive," in *The Encyclopedia of Sexual Behavior*, ed. Albert Ellis & Albert Abarbanel (New York: Hawthorn Books, 1961), Vol. 2, pp. 939–948.
20. Erik H. Erikson, "Inner and Outer Space: Reflections on Womanhood," in *The Woman in America* (Boston: Beacon Press, 1967), pp. 1–26.

five COLLEGE AND AFTER

1. Group for the Advancement of Psychiatry, *Considerations of Personality Development in College Students*, Report No. 32 (New York: GAP, 1955).
2. Matina S. Horner, "Why Women Fail," *Psychology Today*, 3, 6: 36 (1969).
3. David Tresemer, "Fear of Success: Popular, but Unproven," *Psychology Today*, 7, 10: 82–85 (1974).
4. Lois W. Hoffman, "Early Childhood Experiences and Women's Achievement Motives," *Journal of Social Issues*, 28: 129–155 (1972); Matina S. Horner, "Toward an Understanding of Achievement-Related Conflicts in Women," *Journal of Social Issues*, 28: 157–175 (1972).
5. Lois W. Hoffman, "Fear of Success in Males and Females: 1965 and 1971," *Journal of Consulting & Clinical Psychology* 42: 353–358.
6. Carol Nadelson and Malkah T. Notman, "The Woman Physician," *Journal of Medical Education*, 47: 176–183 (1972).

7. Grace K. Baruch, "Maternal Influences upon College Women's Attitudes toward Women and Work," *Developmental Psychology*, 6: 32–37 (1972).
8. James Anthony and Therese Benedek, *Parenthood: Its Psychology and Psychopathology* (Boston: Little, Brown, 1970).
9. Helen H. Tartakoff, "Psychoanalytic Perspectives on Women: Past, Present, and Future," prepared for the conference *Women: Resource for a Changing World*, Radcliffe Institute, April 1972 (Cambridge, Massachusetts: Radcliffe College, 1972).

six PSYCHOTHERAPY AND PSYCHOTHERAPISTS

1. Inge K. Broverman, Susan Raymond Vogel, Donald M. Broverman, F. E. Clarkson, and Paul S. Rosenkrantz, "Sex-Role Stereotypes: A Current Appraisal," *Journal of Social Issues,* 28: 59–78 (1972).
2. Joy K. Rice and David C. Rice, "Implications of the Women's Liberation Movement for Psychotherapy," *American Journal of Psychiatry*, 130: 191–196 (1973).

seven TOWARD CHANGE

1. Gerhart Saenger, "Minority Personality and Adjustment," *Transactions of the New York Academy of Sciences*, 14: 204–208 (1952).
2. John P. McKee and Alex C. Sherriffs, "The Differential Evaluation of Males and Females," *Journal of Personality*, 25: 356–371 (1957).
3. Alex C. Sherriffs and John P. McKee, "Qualitative Aspects of Beliefs about Men and Women," *Journal of Personality*, 25: 450–464 (1957).

4. Kenneth Keniston, "Themes and Conflicts of Autonomous Young Women," 19th Karen Horney Memorial Lecture presented at a meeting of the Association for the Advancement of Psychoanalysis in New York City, March 24, 1971.

5. Alice S. Rossi, "The Roots of Ambivalence in American Women," in *Readings on the Psychology of Women*, ed. Judith M. Bardwick (New York: Harper & Row, 1972), pp. 125–127.

6. Anne Steinmann, J. Levi, and D. Fox, "Self Concept of College Women Compared with Their Concept of Ideal Woman," *Journal of Consulting Psychology*, 11: 370–374 (1964).

7. Keniston, *op. cit.*

8. *Ibid.*

9. *Ibid.*

10. Anne Steinmann, J. Levi, and D. Fox, "Male-Female Perceptions of the Female Role in the United States," *Journal of Psychology*, 64: 265–279 (1966).

11. Matina S. Horner, "Why Women Fail," *Psychology Today*, 3, 6: 36 (1969).

12. *Ibid.*

13. *Ibid.*

14. Joseph Katz, "Coeducational Living: Effects upon Male-Female Relationships," in *Student Development and Education in College Residence Halls*, ed. David A. Decoster and Phyllis L. Mable (Washington, D.C.: American Personnel and Guidance Association, 1974).

15. Joseph Katz, "Coeducational Living on Five College Campuses" (1972, unpublished).

16. Rhona Rapoport and Robert N. Rapoport, "The Dual Career Family," *Human Relations*, 22: 3–30 (1969).

17. Lynda Lytle Holmstrom, "The Two-Career Family," address prepared for the conference *Women: Resource for a Changing World*, Radcliffe Institute, April 1972 (Cambridge, Massachusetts: Radcliffe College, 1972).

18. Rapoport and Rapoport, *op. cit.*

19. Holmstrom, *op. cit.*

20. Paul S. Rosenkrantz, "Egalitarian Families: Some Clinical Observa-

tions," address prepared for the conference *Women: Resource for a Changing World*, Radcliffe Institute, April 1972 (Cambridge, Massachusetts: Radcliffe College, 1972).

21. Nena O'Neill and George O'Neill, *Open Marriage* (New York: Avon Books, 1972).

22. Eugene E. Levitt and Albert D. Klassen, Jr., "Public Attitudes toward Sexual Behaviors: The Latest Investigation of the Institute for Sex Research," *American Journal of Orthopsychiatry*, 43: 285–286 (1973).

23. Katz, "Coeducational Living: Effects upon Male-Female Relationships," *op. cit.*

24. Zella Luria, "Recent Women College Graduates: A Study of Rising Expectations," *American Journal of Orthopsychiatry*, 44: 312–327 (1974).

25. Elizabeth Aub Reid, "Effects of Coresidential Living on the Attitudes, Self-Image, and Role Expectations of College Women," *American Journal of Psychiatry*, 131: 551–554 (1974).

FOR FURTHER READING

Anthony, James, and Benedek, Therese. *Parenthood: Its Psychology and Psychopathology.* Boston: Little, Brown, 1970.

Astin, Helen S. *The Woman Doctorate in America.* New York: Russell Sage Foundation, 1970.

Astin, Helen S., Parelman, Allison, and Fisher, Ann. *Sex Roles: An Annotated Research Bibliography.* Washington, D.C.: Government Printing Office, 1975.

Astin, Helen S., Suniewick, Nancy, and Dweck, Susan. *Women: A Bibliography on Their Education and Careers.* Washington, D.C.: Human Service Press, 1971.

Bardwick, Judith M. *The Psychology of Women.* New York: Harper & Row, 1971.

———, ed. *Readings in the Psychology of Women.* New York: Harper & Row, 1972.

Bernard, Jessie. *Academic Women.* University Park, Pennsylvania: Pennsylvania State University Press, 1964.

———. *The Future of Marriage.* New York: World, 1972.

Bullough, Vern L., and Bullough, Bonnie. *The Subordinate Sex.* Baltimore: Penguin Books, 1974.

Cade, Toni, ed. *The Black Woman.* New York: New American Library, 1970.

Carnegie Commission on Higher Education. *Opportunities for Women in Higher Education.* New York: McGraw-Hill, 1973.

Chafe, William H. *The American Woman.* New York: Oxford University Press, 1972.

Cornillon, Susan K., ed. *Images of Women in Fiction: Feminist Perspectives.* Bowling Green, Ohio: Bowling Green Press, 1972.

Epstein, Cynthia Fuchs. *Woman's Place.* Berkeley, California: University of California Press, 1971.

Farber, Seymour M., and Wilson, Roger H. L., eds. *Man and Civilization: The Potential of Woman; A Symposium.* New York: McGraw-Hill, 1963.

Firestone, Shulamith. *The Dialectic of Sex.* New York: Morrow, 1970.

Franks, Violet, and Burtle, Vasanti. *Women in Therapy.* New York: Brunner/Mazel, 1974.

Fuller, Margaret. *Women in the Nineteenth Century.* New York: W. W. Norton, 1971.

Ginzberg, Eli, and Yohalem, Alice M., eds. *Corporate Lib: Women's Challenge to Management.* Baltimore: Johns Hopkins University Press, 1973.

Gornick, Vivian, and Moran, Barbara K., eds. *Woman in Sexist Society.* New York: Signet Books, 1972.

Greer, Germaine. *The Female Eunuch.* New York: Bantam Books, 1972.

Group for the Advancement of Psychiatry. *Sex and the College Student.* New York: Fawcett World Library, 1966.

Grunebaum, Henry, and Christ, Jacob, eds. *Marriage: Problems and Prospects.* Boston: Little, Brown, 1974.

Huber, Joan, ed. *Changing Women in a Changing Society.* Chicago: University of Chicago Press, 1973.

Janeway, Elizabeth. *Man's World, Woman's Place.* New York: Dell, 1972.

Jencks, Christopher, and Riesman, David. *The Academic Revolution.* Garden City, N.Y.: Doubleday, Anchor Books, 1969.

Kraditor, Aileen S., ed. *Up from the Pedestal.* Chicago: Quadrangle Books, 1968.

Kreps, Juanita. *Sex in the Marketplace: American Women at Work.* Baltimore: Johns Hopkins University Press, 1971.

Kundsin, Ruth, ed. *Women and Success.* New York: Morrow, 1974.

Lifton, Robert Jay, ed. *The Woman in America.* Boston: Beacon Press, 1967.

Maccoby, Eleanor E., ed. *The Development of Sex Differences.* Stanford, Calif.: Stanford University Press, 1966.

Maccoby, Eleanor Emmons, and Jacklin, Carol Nagy. *Psychology of Sex Differences.* Stanford, Calif.: Stanford University Press, 1974.

Masters, William H., and Johnson, Virginia E. *Human Sexual Response.* Boston: Little, Brown, 1966.

Mead, Margaret. *Male and Female.* New York: William Morrow, 1949.

Mill, John Stuart, and Mill, Harriet Taylor. *Essays on Sexual Equality,* ed. Alice S. Rossi. Chicago: University of Chicago Press, 1970.

Miller, Jean Baker, ed. *Psychoanalysis and Women.* Baltimore: Penguin Books, 1973.

Millett, Kate. *Sexual Politics.* New York: Avon Books, 1971.

Mitchell, Juliet. *Psychoanalysis and Feminism.* New York: Pantheon Books, 1974.

———. *Women's Estate.* New York: Random House, Vintage Books, 1973.

Money, John, and Ehrhardt, Anke A. *Man and Woman, Boy and Girl.* Baltimore: Johns Hopkins University Press, 1972.

Morgan, Robin, ed. *Sisterhood is Powerful.* New York: Random House, Vintage Books, 1970).

Nye, F. Ivan, and Hoffman, Lois W., eds. *The Employed Mother in America.* Chicago: Rand McNally, 1963.

Rapoport, Rhona, and Rapoport, Robert N. *Dual Career Families.* Baltimore: Penguin Books, 1971.

Reid, Inez Smith. *"Together" Black Women.* New York: Emerson Books, 1972.

Rosenbaum, Salo, and Alger, Ian, eds. *The Marriage Relationship.* New York: Basic Books, 1968.

Rossi, Alice S., ed. *The Feminist Papers.* New York: Bantam Books, 1974.

Schaeffer, Dirk L., ed. *Sex Differences in Personality Readings.* Belmont, California: Brooks/Cole, 1971.

Sherfey, Mary Jane. *The Nature and Evolution of Female Sexuality.* New York: Random House, Vintage Books, 1973.

Stoller, Robert J. *Sex and Gender.* New York: Science House, 1968.

Westervelt, Esther Manning, and Fixter, Deborah A. *Women's Higher and Continuing Education: An Annotated Bibliography with Selected References on Related Aspects of Women's Lives.* New York: College Entrance Examination Board, 1971.

Women: Resource for a Changing World. Conference, Radcliffe Institute, April 1972 (Cambridge, Massachusetts: Radcliffe College, 1972).

Zubin, Joseph, and Money, John, eds. *Contemporary Sexual Behavior: Critical Issues in the 1970's.* Baltimore: Johns Hopkins University Press, 1973.

SOME PSYCHOANALYTIC WRITINGS

Chasseguet-Smirgel, Janine. *Female Sexuality.* Ann Arbor, Michigan: University of Michigan Press, 1970.

Deutsch, Helene. *Psychology of Women.* 2 vols. New York: Bantam Books, 1973.

Erikson, Erik. *Childhood and Society.* New York: W. W. Norton, 1963.

———. *Identity and the Life Cycle.* Psychological Issues. New York: International Universities Press, 1959.

————. *Identity: Youth and Crisis*. New York: W. W. Norton, 1968.

Freud, Anna. *The Ego and the Mechanisms of Defense*. London: Hogarth Press, 1942.

Freud, Sigmund. *New Introductory Lectures on Psychoanalysis*, ed. James Strachey. New York: W. W. Norton, 1965.

————. *Sexuality and the Psychology of Love*, ed. Philip Rieff. New York: Collier Books, 1963.

Harding, M. Esther. *The Way of All Women*. New York: G. P. Putnam's Sons; for the C. G. Jung Foundation for Analytical Psychology, 1970.

Horney, Karen. *Feminine Psychology*, ed. Harold Kelman. New York: W. W. Norton, 1973.

Jung, C. G. "Marriage as a Psychological Relationship," *Collected Works*, vol. 17, Bollingen Series XX. Princeton, N.J.: Princeton University Press, 1970.

Jung, Emma. *Animus and Anima*. Zurich, Switzerland: Spring Publications, 1972.

Scott-Maxwell, Florida. *Women and Sometimes Men*. New York: Alfred Knopf, 1957.

INDEX

sexual development, stages of, 57
sexual equality, growing acceptance of, 39, 60
sexual expression, relationship to love feelings, 76–77
sexual feelings, focus of, 77
sexual identity, ambiguity as a concept, 54, 56
sexual orientation
  changing attitudes toward, 135–136, 137–138
  definition of, 56
  development of, 62, 67, 74, 82, 86
  differing opportunities for, 83–84
Sexual Politics (Millet), 31
sexual response
  determination of, 59–60, 74, 75
  research on, 74–77
sexual responsiveness, development of, 86
sexual revolution, 31
single state, deliberate choice of, 136–137
Smith, Sophia, 24–25
Smith College, 22, 24–25
smoking, public acceptance of, 27
socialization process, 44–45, 58
social reformer, role of, 24–25
social structure, feminist view of, 34
social values, changes in, 144–145
Stanton, Elizabeth Cady, 24
Steinmann, Anne, 121, 124
Stone, Lucy, 24
Stowe, Harriet Beecher, 25

success
  ambivalent feelings toward, 47, 49, 88–89, 93, 124–127
  changing concepts of, 126, 144, 151
sulfa drugs, social impact of, 28
Superman image, 68
symbiotic relationship, 63

Tarbell, Ida R., 25
teachers, psychological influence of, 17–18, 36–37
therapist, unconscious influence of, 113–116
Thomas, M. Carey, 25
trade union movement, 25–26
two-career family
  conflicts of, 41, 130–134
  growing acceptance of, 128, 129, 149–150

unconscious feelings
  development of, 64, 65, 121
  effect of, 45, 47, 50
  influence of, 86, 89, 97–98
unisex style, 32, 60
United States Constitution, 24, 32

Vassar College, 22
venereal disease, fear of, 28, 31
Victorianism, social attitudes of, 21, 22, 25–27

Wald, Lillian D., 25
Wellesley College, 22, 143
Willard, Frances, 25
"Woman in America, The," 31
woman suffrage movement, 20, 23–24, 25–26

women's colleges, establishment of, 22–23
women's liberation movement, 20, 37, 119, 122
women's movement. *See* feminist movement
Women's Studies, need for, 141

World War I, social impact of, 27
World War II, social impact of, 28, 29
writer, role of, 21

Zero Population Growth, 81

GAP COMMITTEES, MEMBERS, AND OFFICERS
(as of January 1, 1975)

COMMITTEES

ADOLESCENCE
Joseph D. Noshpitz, Washington, D.C.,
  Chairman
Maurice R. Friend, New York, N.Y.
Warren J. Gadpaille, Englewood, Colo.
Charles A. Malone, Philadelphia, Pa.
Silvio J. Onesti, Jr., Belmont, Mass.
Jeanne Spurlock, Silver Spring, Md.
Sidney L. Werkman, Denver, Colo.

AGING
Prescott W. Thompson, San Jose, Calif.,
  Chairman
Robert N. Butler, Washington, D.C.
Charles M. Gaitz, Houston, Tex.
Alvin I. Goldfarb, New York, N.Y.
Lawrence F. Greenleigh, Los Angeles,
  Calif.
Maurice E. Linden, Philadelphia, Pa.
Robert D. Patterson, Lexington, Mass.
F. Conyers Thompson, Jr., Atlanta, Ga.
Montague Ullman, Ardsley, N.Y.
Jack Weinberg, Chicago, Ill.

CHILD PSYCHIATRY
Joseph M. Green, Tucson, Ariz., *Chairman*
Paul L. Adams, Miami, Fla.
E. James Anthony, St. Louis, Mo.

James M. Bell, Canaan, N.Y.
Harlow Donald Dunton, New York,
  N.Y.
Joseph Fischoff, Detroit, Mich.
John F. Kenward, Chicago, Ill.
Ake Mattsson, Charlottesville, Va.
John F. McDermott, Jr., Honolulu, Hawaii
Theodore Shapiro, New York, N.Y.
Exie E. Welsch, New York, N.Y.
Virginia N. Wilking, New York, N.Y.

THE COLLEGE STUDENT
Robert L. Arnstein, Hamden, Conn.
  Chairman
Harrison P. Eddy, New York, N.Y.
Malkah Tolpin Notman, Brookline,
  Mass.
Gloria C. Onque, Pittsburgh, Pa.
Kent E. Robinson, Towson, Md.
Earle Silber, Chevy Chase, Md.
Tom G. Stauffer, White Plains, N.Y.

THE FAMILY
Joseph Satten, San Francisco, Calif.,
  Chairman
C. Christian Beels, Bronx, N.Y.
Ivan Boszormenyi-Nagy, Wyncote, Pa.
Murray Bowen, Chevy Chase, Md.

183

184

185

Andrew P. Morrison, Cambridge, Mass.
William C. Offenkrantz, Chicago, Ill.
William L. Peltz, Manchester, Vt.
Franz K. Reichsman, Brooklyn, N.Y.
Lewis L. Robbins, Glen Oaks, N.Y.

Richard I. Shader, Newton Centre, Mass.
Harley C. Shands, New York, N.Y.
Joseph P. Tupin, Sacramento, Calif.
Herbert Weiner, Bronx, N.Y.

MEMBERS

CONTRIBUTING MEMBERS
Carlos C. Alden, Jr., Buffalo, N.Y.
Charlotte G. Babcock, Pittsburgh, Pa.
Grace Baker, New York, N.Y.
Walter E. Barton, Washington, D.C.
Spencer Bayles, Houston, Tex.
Anne R. Benjamin, Chicago, Ill.
Ivan C. Berlien, Coral Gables, Fla.
Sidney Berman, Washington, D.C.
Grete L. Bibring, Cambridge, Mass.
Edward G. Billings, Denver, Colo.
Carl A. L. Binger, Cambridge, Mass.
H. Waldo Bird, St. Louis, Mo.
Wilfred Bloomberg, Boston, Mass.
H. Keith H. Brodie, Baltimore, Md.
Eugene Brody, Menlo Park, Calif.
Matthew Brody, Brooklyn, N.Y.
Ewald W. Busse, Durham, N.H.
Dale Cameron, Guilford, Conn.
Gerald Caplan, Boston, Mass.
Hugh T. Carmichael, Washington, D.C.
Ian L. W. Clancey, Maitland, Ontario, Canada
Sanford I. Cohen, Boston, Mass.
Jules V. Coleman, New Haven, Conn.
Robert Coles, Cambridge, Mass.
Frank J. Curran, New York, N.Y.
William D. Davidson, Washington, D.C.
Leonard J. Duhl, Berkeley, Calif.
Joel Elkes, Baltimore, Md.
Joseph T. English, New York, N.Y.
Louis C. English, Pomona, N.Y.
O. Spurgeon English, Narberth, Pa.
Dana L. Farnsworth, Boston, Mass.
Stuart M. Finch, Tucson, Ariz.
Alfred Flarsheim, Chicago, Ill.

Archie R. Foley, New York, N.Y.
Alan Frank, Albuquerque, N.M.
Daniel X. Freedman, Chicago, Ill.
Albert J. Glass, Chicago, Ill.
Louis A. Gottschalk, Irvine, Calif.
Milton Greenblatt, Sepulveda, Calif.
Maurice H. Greenhill, Scarsdale, N.Y.
John H. Greist, Indianapolis, Ind.
Roy R. Grinker, Sr., Chicago, Ill.
Ernest M. Gruenberg, Poughkeepsie, N.Y.
Edward O. Harper, Cleveland, Ohio
Mary O'Neill Hawkins, New York, N.Y.
J. Cotter Hirschberg, Topeka, Kans.
Edward J. Hornick, New York, N.Y.
Joseph Hughes, Philadelphia, Pa.
Portia Bell Hume, Berkeley, Calif.
Irene M. Josselyn, Phoenix, Ariz.
Jay Katz, New Haven, Conn.
Sheppard G. Kellam, Chicago, Ill.
Marion E. Kenworthy, New York, N.Y.
Gerald L. Klerman, Boston, Mass.
Othilda M. Krug, Cincinnati, Ohio
Zigmond M. Lebensohn, Washington, D.C.
Henry D. Lederer, Washington, D.C.
Robert L. Leopold, Philadelphia, Pa.
Alan I. Levenson, Tucson, Ariz.
Earl A. Loomis, New York, N.Y.
Reginald S. Lourie, Washington, D.C.
Alfred O. Ludwig, Boston, Mass.
Jeptha R. MacFarlane, Westbury, N.Y.
John A. MacLeod, Cincinnati, Ohio
Sidney G. Margolin, Denver, Colo.
Helen V. McLean, Chicago, Ill.
Jack H. Mendelson, Belmont, Mass.

Karl A. Menninger, Topeka, Kans.
James G. Miller, Louisville, Ky.
John A. P. Millet, Nyack, N.Y.
Peter B. Neubauer, New York, N.Y.
Rudolph G. Novick, Lincolnwood, Ill.
Lucy D. Ozarin, Bethesda, Md.
Irving Philips, San Francisco, Calif.
Charles A. Pinderhughes, Boston, Mass.
Eveoleen N. Rexford, Cambridge, Mass.
Milton Rosenbaum, Bronx, N.Y.
W. Donald Ross, Cincinnati, Ohio
Lester H. Rudy, Chicago, Ill.
David S. Sanders, Beverly Hills, Calif.
Kurt O. Schlesinger, San Francisco, Calif.
Elvin V. Semrad, Boston, Mass.
Calvin F. Settlage, Sausalito, Calif.
Benson R. Snyder, Cambridge, Mass.
John P. Spiegel, Waltham, Mass.
Brandt F. Steele, Denver, Colo.
Eleanor A. Steele, Denver, Colo.
Rutherford B. Stevens, New York, N.Y.
Alan A. Stone, Cambridge, Mass.
Perry C. Talkington, Dallas, Tex.
Graham C. Taylor, Montreal, Canada
Lloyd J. Thompson, Chapel Hill, N.C.

Harvey J. Tompkins, New York, N.Y.
Lucia E. Tower, Chicago, Ill.
Arthur F. Valenstein, Cambridge, Mass.
Suzanne T. van Amerongen, Boston, Mass.
Harold M. Visotsky, Chicago, Ill.
Robert S. Wallerstein, San Francisco, Calif.
Andrew S. Watson, Ann Arbor, Mich.
Edward M. Weinshel, San Francisco, Calif.
Joseph B. Wheelwright, San Francisco, Calif.
Robert L. Williams, Houston, Tex.
David G. Wright, Providence, R.I.
Stanley F. Yolles, Stony Brook, N.Y.

LIFE MEMBERS
S. Spafford Ackerly, Louisville, Ky.
Kenneth E. Appel, Ardmore, Pa.
Malcolm J. Farrell, Waverley, Mass.
William S. Langford, New York, N.Y.
Benjamin Simon, Boston, Mass.
Francis H. Sleeper, Augusta, Maine

LIFE CONSULTANT
Mrs. Ethel L. Ginsburg, New York, N.Y.

BOARD OF DIRECTORS

President: Judd Marmor
Vice President: John C. Nemiah
Secretary: Jack A. Wolford
Treasurer: Gene L. Usdin
Immediate Past President: George Tarjan

MEMBERS
C. Knight Aldrich
Viola W. Bernard
Robert N. Butler
Leo Madow
Charles B. Wilkinson

Honorary Member: Malcolm J. Farrell

PAST PRESIDENTS, EX-OFFICIO	
Jack R. Ewalt	1951–53
Walter E. Barton	1953–55
Dana L. Farnsworth	1957–59
Marion E. Kenworthy	1959–61
Henry W. Brosin	1961–63
Leo H. Bartemeier	1963–65
Robert S. Garber	1965–67
Herbert C. Modlin	1967–69
John Donnelly	1969–71

DECEASED PAST PRESIDENTS	
William C. Menninger	1946–51
Sol W. Ginsburg	1955–57

188